your
DNA
guide
the book

your DNA guide
the book

Step-by-step plans
to connect you with your family using your DNA

By Diahan Southard

Printed in the United States of America

ISBN 978-1-7346139-0-2 Print

ISBN 978-1-7346139-1-9 eBook

Your DNA Guide
724.484.3344
www.yourDNAguide.com

I would like to dedicate this, my very first book, to my parents. Because of them it has never occurred to me that I couldn't do or have or be whatever I wanted.

And to my husband. The man who was the first to demand that I just be me, and loved me for it.

Acknowledgments

While this book represents my work and I am solely responsible for its content, much of what happens in the Your DNA Guide world is a result of teamwork with other excellent experts. The following experts have chimed in to write these sections of the book: Jayne Ekins, *Pedigree Collapse* and Sunny Jane Morton, *Genealogy Research*.

Also, thank you to my friend and editor Sunny Morton for helping to get this book out of my head and into print, and for fixing all my run-ons and en (or is it em?) dashes.

Thank you to beta readers Katie Ritchie, Christi Jacobsen, Angie Bush, Kathie Knoll, Christine Ellin, Linda Smith, JoAnn Hertzler, Drew Smith, Pat Gordon and James Beidler (my adopted dad).

I would also like to recognize the significant work of my colleagues in the genetic genealogy industry, as their ideas and methodologies have certainly influenced the way I think about and use genetic genealogy.

There is no question that I would not be where I am today without Scott Woodward, PhD and the Sorenson Molecular Genealogy Foundation. Scott's vision and passion for this field was utterly contagious and has forever shaped my future.

Ugo A. Perego, PhD was an early and influential mentor. He and Anna Swayne, formerly of AncestryDNA, believed in me early and often. Anna would go on to introduce me to key people within her professional circles that accelerated my acceptance as an industry leader. We grew up in this DNA world together and I consider them my earliest supporters and dearest friends.

Blaine Bettinger, PhD, JD has been not only an expert thought-leader in the genetic genealogy industry, but is generous with his expertise and mentoring. Judy G. Russell, JD, has inspired me with her expert knowledge about literally everything and her engaging skill as a presenter. Angie Bush, genetic genealogy expert and a senior genealogist with Ancestry ProGenealogists, has been one of my biggest cheerleaders, and my go-to girl for any questions I come across.

intro

working your plan

learning guides

Ready. Set. Go!

intro to your plan

things you need to know

Before you dive into your own customized DNA Plan, let's have a little chat. Let me warn you right off the bat: *It works*. That means that before you start, you need to understand that you will likely find what you are looking for. If not right away, then eventually. So make sure you really want to know before we go poking around in your DNA.

This DNA technology is powerful, and it has the ability to transform the way you see yourself and your family members. You may think you are doing it to understand one family mystery, and in the process uncover a few others. Depending on the ancestor you are looking for, and the information you find, your discovery could change the relationships of those around you. Your DNA doesn't just speak for you; it speaks for everyone you are related to. Keep in mind: once you know, you can't unknow.

How's that for a pep talk? For those of you who haven't placed this book firmly back on the shelf and turned on Netflix, let's start putting your DNA to work for you.

an overview

To get good, specific answers from your DNA, you need to ask good, specific questions, and then go about answering them in a logical, systematic fashion. Each time you come to your DNA with something on your mind, you'll need to create and follow a Plan that includes these steps:

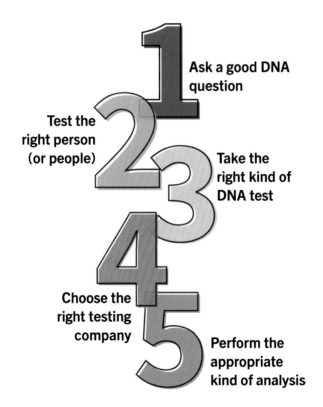

1 Ask a good DNA question

Test the right person (or people)

3 Take the right kind of DNA test

Choose the right testing company

5 Perform the appropriate kind of analysis

Don't panic if this process seems daunting. *The entire purpose of this book is to teach you how to do this.* So aren't you glad you bought this book? So go ahead and let out that breath you were just holding and keep reading.

Ask a Good DNA Question

I am guessing you bought this book because you have some kind of question you want your DNA to answer. Are you trying to bust down that 20-year genealogical brick wall? Or maybe you just have a vague thought of, "I want to learn more about my roots" or "What in the world do I do with the information in my DNA test?" Either of these questions is a good start, but you need to break it down a little more. If you don't, it is like walking into a genealogy library, taking a book off the shelf, and leafing through it hoping to find something that relates to your family. It's just not going to happen. (Or if it does, put down the book and go out and buy a lottery ticket: it's your lucky day!)

A good DNA question is one that is **specific** and that's **appropriate** to ask your DNA.

Specific: While your DNA may be able to help you answer questions about your ethnic origins, this book will focus on how your DNA can help you identify actual family relationships. Some questions this book can help you answer would be:

Who is my biological parent?

Am I interpreting my results correctly? (Especially results that may be unexpected or unwelcome)

Who is my unidentified ancestor (a biological grandparent, great-grandparent, etc)?

How am I related to this mystery match on my DNA match list?

Appropriate: As much as we would like it to be, DNA is not a crystal ball. The most appropriate questions will focus on generations closer than your 4X great grandparents, and will ask not for the names of specific ancestors, but just good genealogy leads and next steps.

Test the Right Person

I am going to assume you have had your own DNA tested already. But even though it doesn't sound very nice, you need to know: *you are likely not enough.* There, I said it. Of course, what I mean by that is: *your DNA test alone may not be enough* to find the answers you want.

It is going to be infinitely easier to answer your question if you have tested the oldest generation possible. What do I mean by that? I mean that when we are talking genealogy and DNA, if both of your parents are alive and willing to be tested, you are genetically irrelevant, as you only have half of your parents' DNA.

If you have a parent or grandparent or aunt or uncle who is related to the ancestor you are researching who wouldn't mind donating some of their saliva to your cause, put this book down right now, and go order them a DNA test. As you move forward through this book, you'll learn more strategies for identifying people to test whose results might be helpful for specific kinds of questions. And you'll even get suggestions for how to locate their contact information and how to successfully invite them to test.

Take the Right Test

Unless we say otherwise, we will be talking exclusively in this book about the kind of DNA test you can take from testing companies like 23andMe, AncestryDNA, Family Tree DNA, MyHeritage DNA, and Living DNA. These companies test DNA that comes from both of your parents, and is referred to as autosomal DNA, sometimes abbreviated as atDNA. You get half of your atDNA from your mom, and half from your dad. Testing this DNA gives you two different kinds of results: maps and percentages that tell you where your ancestors may have come from, and a DNA match list showing you other people who have taken the test, that likely share a common ancestor within a genealogical timeframe (like the last 500 years or so).

Depending on your DNA questions, two other kinds of DNA tests may prove valuable. If the ancestor you are looking for is a male, head over to page 232 to determine whether YDNA may be a good fit for your question. If the ancestor you are seeking is female, you may want to read the mtDNA section on page 184 for tips on when that might be valuable.

Choose the Right Company

Several different companies offer autosomal DNA testing for family history purposes. Each has different strengths and weaknesses. For example, 23andMe is best known for the health reports it offers with its Health + Ancestry test (although you can just purchase the ancestry part, and other testing companies now have health report products, too).

Ancestry's testing pool is currently THE largest—well over 15 million—but plenty of people have tested elsewhere, including at MyHeritage, which because of its market focus outside the United States may be a better place for some people to find DNA matches in Europe, the Middle East and elsewhere. The testing pool at 23andMe is very large—the only one

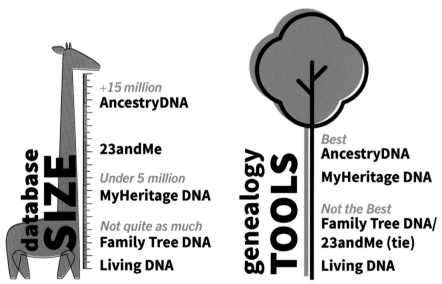

database SIZE

+15 million
AncestryDNA

23andMe

Under 5 million
MyHeritage DNA

Not quite as much
Family Tree DNA

Living DNA

genealogy TOOLS

Best
AncestryDNA

MyHeritage DNA

Not the Best
**Family Tree DNA/
23andMe (tie)**

Living DNA

currently comparable to AncestryDNA's in size—and that's important because a larger testing pool increases your odds of finding close genetic matches who have also tested at that site. However, at 23andMe many have not opted into matching, which means they won't be showing up on your DNA match list.

Ancestry and MyHeritage have the most robust tools for comparing (and even researching) your family trees right there on their sites, followed by Family Tree DNA (FTDNA) and 23andMe (I'd give them a tie) and then Living DNA. Family Tree DNA also offers mitochondrial and YDNA testing, and has user-run projects for comparing large groups of people who share DNA (like a common surname or place of origin), so is a good place for those who like the idea of one-stop shopping and these more advanced options. But keep in mind that the database at FTDNA is very small compared to the other sites. It is also important to keep in mind that FTDNA has a partnership with law enforcement and anyone in the US who tests there is automatically opted into that law enforcement search unless they specifically turn off that feature in their account. Those outside of the United States and covered by GDPR will be presented with the choice to opt-in upon activation of their DNA kit.

As if this isn't enough variety to consider, each testing company also calculates its ethnicity regions differently and with different levels of detail in various parts of the world (for example, Living DNA breaks down British Isles descent into 21 detailed categories). Most companies retail their DNA kits for about $99 (those are US dollars). But my advice when buying breakfast cereal also applies to DNA kits: Never pay full price. So take a quick look at the nearest calendar and see if there is some kind of holiday coming up.

A chart comparing precise numbers and details for each of these testing companies would become out of date within weeks, so instead of including it in this book, it's in my Autosomal DNA quick reference guide, which I update regularly (you can buy the current print or digital download version at www.yourdnaguide.com/quick-guides).

The very best way to be absolutely sure you aren't missing any matches or insights is to test with every company. If it's within your budget and you consider it a worthwhile investment, go for it. But that isn't possible for everyone. Currently the most economical way to test a new person is to test first with AncestryDNA, and then transfer their DNA data to MyHeritage, Family Tree DNA, and Living DNA, all of which allow uploads of your DNA test results from other companies. AncestryDNA doesn't allow anyone to transfer their results into their database. (For full instructions on transferring, see www.yourDNAguide.com/transferring).

While you are shopping on the internet for your DNA tests, if you feel like you made out like a bandit with all those savings, you may consider testing multiple relatives. You really can't ever have too much data. This is especially true if you are going to be looking for a great-grandparent, or a great-great-grandparent. Testing as many descendants of that ancestor as possible is the key. Check out the section on targeted testing for more ideas (page 224). But I am getting ahead of myself.

Why physically test at more than one company? There are some definite advantages to actually physically testing at each company. One big reason to do this is that we just don't know what the future holds. (At least, I don't. If you do, well, I guess you can skip this whole exercise and just look ahead to the part where you find out the answer to your question.) In five or ten years there will be new technologies and new ways to look at our DNA. If your physical DNA sample doesn't reside with the company that comes up with that next big thing, well, you may miss out. When you think of it like a DNA banking service, the $49 - $99 investment doesn't seem so bad.

Perform the proper analysis

Your test results don't usually scream out the direct answer to your specific question (there are exceptions). After getting your results, you will usually need to examine them. You may need to sift, filter, eliminate, cluster, triangulate, construct, etc. Again: this book is here with step-by-step instructions for whatever your next step will be. It's laid out kind of like those *Choose Your Own Adventure* books I grew up reading. When you identify what you want to do next, you'll skip to the section that explains that step, and then I'll send you along to whatever will come next after that. (What this also tells you is that you don't need to read this book straight through—although you're welcome to—but just skip around to the parts that apply to your current DNA question as directed by your Plan.)

 Are you ready to move on?

1. I have formulated a good DNA question.

2. I've chosen appropriate people to test for this question, which includes all the oldest living generations in my family.

3. I've chosen an appropriate test type and testing company to address my question.

4. I've got a firm grip on this book, because it's going to guide me through the process of answering my questions.

10

Great! Let's keep going.

family tree

OK, so you have now made sure that you have tested all of the right people. But before you start looking for unknown people in your family tree, you need to make sure you are ready to take full advantage of your DNA test. That means you need to have at least a small family tree (if you are new to all of this tree-making, see page 155), attach your family tree to your DNA test results, and be sure it's a public tree. This gives you and your match helpful clues to better understand your relationship. At Ancestry and MyHeritage, this will also activate several useful tools that can significantly help you in your search.

This tree does not have to be the tree you have been building for 20 years that contains every picture and every document you have ever collected. Many people opt for a DNA tree, which is just the bare bones of their tree (names, relationships, and birth/death dates and places), without any of the extra fun stuff.

For tips on building the best possible family tree for your DNA testing experience, go to the Genealogy Research section of this book on page 155. For instructions on how to attach a family tree to your results at each testing company, go to www.yourdnaguide.com/resources and choose your testing company.

As you proceed with your research, you may find yourself learning new names, dates, places and other details from relatives or through genealogy research. Make sure you update the family tree that's attached to your DNA results.

Are you ready to move on?

1. I've got a family tree that represents my entire family to the best of my knowledge, and especially documents as much as I know about the branch of my family I will be tackling.

2. I've attached a family tree to my DNA results.

3. I've read the Genealogy Research section of this book (page 155) for tips on how to improve my tree for DNA analysis, and I'll update the tree I've attached to my DNA test as needed.

4. The tree I attach to my DNA results doesn't have to be my full tree with lots of photos and documents. It just needs to have the names, dates and places that will help identify common ancestors (when compared to someone else's tree).

12

ancestral ethnicity results

For most people, the first stop in their DNA journey is the ethnicity pie chart: maps and percentages that describe how much of their DNA is from where. While I used to consider these to be a mere coffee table piece, your biogeographical ancestry maps (as they are also known) have significantly improved in the last couple of years. This is due to ongoing refinements in three of the factors that affect your results: reference populations, fancy math, and timing. Read about those below, but understand that not all companies are doing this equally well. The clear leaders are AncestryDNA and 23andMe, with MyHeritage DNA and Living DNA close behind, with Family Tree DNA in a very distant last. Another important take-home for you is that you will likely see updates periodically. So every now and then, log back in to see what changes have been made, then use what you learn below to understand why.

Reference Populations

One of the biggest factors in these calculations are the reference populations used by the testing companies. Reference populations are groups of people who have been chosen to genetically represent a population. In short, if a testing company doesn't have a good representation of the ancestral location you are trying to find, it may not show up in your DNA.

Additionally, because there is so much genetic overlap between neighboring countries, sometimes your German DNA gets sucked into your British Isles category, or your British ancestry gets siphoned off to your Scandinavian category.

Fancy Math

This brings up the Fancy Math aspect of these results.

It seems like it should be a fairly simple process: test a group of Irish people to find out what Irish DNA looks like. If someone who is tested has that same Irish DNA, we assign them to the Irish category. However, it is just way more complicated than that. It has to do with likelihoods and probabilities, with the root problem being the simple fact that we are all, on some level, actually related to each other.

Timing

 The last factor is timing. Your DNA test may show that you have some Middle Eastern DNA, and it may even be real — meaning that you do have origins in that part of the world. The big question is when? When did you have ancestors there? If it was more than a thousand years ago, you will likely never find any genealogical evidence (and here I am talking about historical records) of your connection to that place.

AncestryDNA's Genetic Communities

All that said, testing companies are getting much much better at helping us actually do genealogy with clues from biogeographical ancestry results. Probably the best example of this is in AncestryDNA's Genetic Communities. These are extremely accurate groupings that are based on both genetics and genealogy and reflect locations that absolutely (and I am not using that word lightly here) should be represented in your family history in the last 200 years. So before you even begin this search for your missing ancestor(s), take a look at your Genetic Communities if you tested at AncestryDNA. If you are a member of any Community that is currently not in your family tree, it's time to take notes. It is very likely that one of your missing branches was standing on that very soil in the not-too-distant past.

Here's a good example: One of our clients here at Your DNA Guide was looking for a great-grandfather: one of those men who seems to show up in Pennsylvania long enough to get married and have a couple kids, but doesn't seem to exist before or after. However, our client was showing a connection to a New Jersey genetic community, and didn't have any other ties to that location in her family tree. As we worked through her Plan, we began to see matches with common connections to—you guessed it—New Jersey! So these maps and percentages are no longer just a coffee table piece, they may be THE piece that puts you on the path to discovering your missing ancestor.

So, go ahead, go take a look. Do you have any Genetic Communities that are suspiciously conspicuous? You do? Perfect. Write down that location and watch for it as we continue with your Plan.

No Genetic Communities? No worries, not everyone has them. You didn't really expect your ancestor, after all these years, to make it easy for you, did you?

23andMe Administrative Regions

The most important part of your Ancestry Composition results at 23andMe are their increasingly small administrative regions. This is where they are breaking down your larger continental categories into smaller, and theoretically more accurate, regions. For example, in the French and German category, there are seven regions, with one of those being Germany. Then under Germany, there are 16 administrative regions where they can assign you to based on your DNA. Pay attention to those regions, as they may contain valuable information regarding the ancestral location of your ancestors.

So long story short, while you certainly should include a glance at your maps and percentages when you are looking for a particular ancestor, the ethnicity results may be just a short stop on your journey. For some, it's more of a sightseeing tour, really, just to be sure there isn't something blatantly obvious in your results that could provide a potential lead early on in our process. For others there will be some big clues that will help you as you work through your Plan. But don't worry, the step-by-step guides later in this book will tell you when it will be important to dig into your ethnicity results for clues.

Checklist: Are you ready to move on?

1.   I've reviewed my ethnicity results for any surprises.

2.   I understand that ancestral ethnicity percentages are not necessarily precise or entirely accurate, but that they are gradually becoming better.

3. If I've tested at AncestryDNA, I've reviewed my Genetic Communities for unfamiliar locations.

4. I realize that I may come back to my ethnicity results when I have specific questions on which they may shed light.

staying organized

As you proceed with your DNA testing Plan, you'll want to make sure you stay focused on your question and document what you learn along the way. Consider creating a document (or notebook, if you're the pen-and-paper type) with your DNA question along the top of the page, the steps you're taking (who you're testing, etc), what analysis you're doing and what it's telling you. Programs like Microsoft OneNote or Evernote make it easy to take screenshots of important information. Update what you learn in every research session.

Throughout your Plan I will refer to specific opportunities to stay organized and on track. Here's a quick list of the relevant resource sections. You may want to quickly review them before you start to make sure you are ready to hit the ground running.

Creating a DNA Research Log (page 199): Essential for any research project to keep yourself on track and remember what you have already learned.

Drawing on Your Match's Pedigree (page 128): Helps you identify important elements of your relationship and sets you up for future success in finding your common ancestor.

Using the Notes Field: Every testing company allows you to take notes about a match right in their site. Use the note fields early and often.

Labeling DNA matches (page 176): Doing this will help document how each match is related to you (as you figure it out). A good label can help you see at-a-glance who your common ancestor is, whether you've communicated with each other, or whatever you most want to remember about this match.

tips for working within your Plan

This book will provide a completely customized Plan to track your DNA journey from your question to your answer. In addition to these Plans, you will need a bunch of patience (with yourself and the process), some serious tenacity, and probably a few lucky breaks.

You might notice that the sections in *Working Your Plan* seem to be named randomly. Well, you are right, they are not given in numerical order. That is because while you will be taken step-by-step, sometimes you need to go right before you can go left, and that just doesn't lend itself to consecutive numbering. So the numbers are there just to help you quickly find a section in the book. There is order to this process: it just isn't in a straight line. The lettering refers to one of five categories of steps: Known Matches (KM), Mystery Matches (MM), Genetic Networks (GN), Doing Genealogy (DG), and Next Steps (NS).

The back section of the book contains the resources and explanations that most everyone will need regardless of their particular question or journey.

So that means you will need a bookmark handy as you skip back and forth between the detailed step-by-step Plans sections and these resources. For example, as part of your Plan you may need to learn a bit about how to use the total amount of shared DNA between you and a match. So you would flip back to that section in the resources, read it (love it!) and then turn back to your Plan for any customized comments on that particular topic that pertain to your individual search.

On the other hand, wandering through the resources is bound to be fun, educational, and insightful, so don't let me stop you!

the map

I know it looks a little crazy, but this is an overview of the steps in the Plan and how they all fit together. Hopefully this will help you see where you are, and where you need to go.

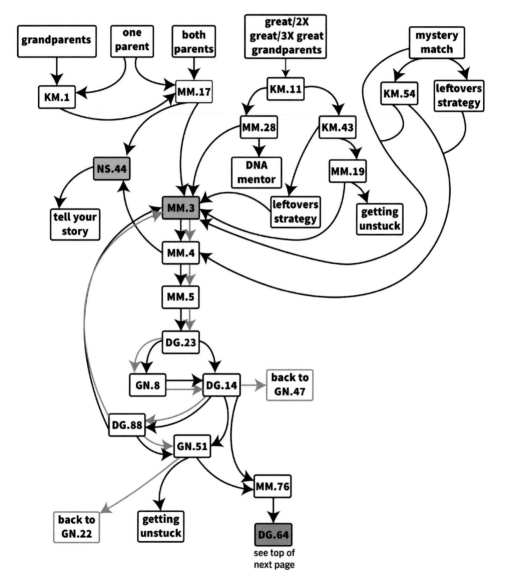

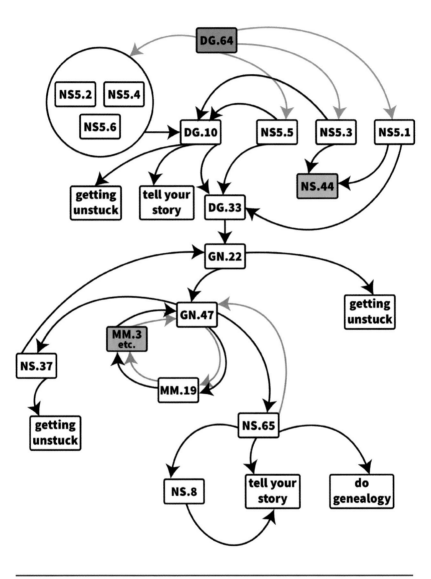

20

Key:

KM = Known Match   GN = Genetic Network   NS = Next Steps

MM = Mystery Match   DG = Doing Genealogy

working your plan

the basic process

For all of the new vocabulary and science-y ideas, genetic genealogy can be boiled down to the need to master a few simple ideas. No matter who you are looking for, from your father to your 2X great grandfather, the process to find them is the same basic four concepts. OK, so it is a little bit more complicated than that, as there are all kinds of caveats and what–ifs and possible rabbit holes to fall down. But overall, if you understand how to apply these four concepts, you will at the very least have a better understanding of what clues can be found in your DNA, and therefore have a better idea of where to go next.

Concept 1: Best Known Matches

See how we are starting out easy? Known matches are those people on your match list for whom you already know your relationship, or to whom

you can easily find your relationship. At first these matches may seem unimportant. After all, you are out to solve a mystery, not be told things you already know. But these known matches are your first key to finding out about unknown matches.

You may have all kinds of known matches in your DNA match list. A Best Known Match is someone who has a documented

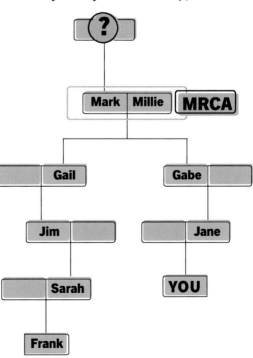

relationship to the ancestor you are trying to find. Since I think you need to read that again, I am going to say it again, but louder and slower: **A Best Known Match is someone who has a documented relationship to the ancestor you are trying to find.** The best Best Known Match is someone whose MRCA (page 235) is the ancestor you are trying to research.

If you are looking for the parents of your great grandfather Mark, then your Best Known Match would be someone else who is a descendant of one of Mark's other children (NOT through his son Gabe, who is your ancestor). When you are related through a different child, that makes Mark (and his wife) your most recent common ancestor (MRCA). Don't skip over that last point. It is very important to identify your MRCA. In all actuality, for most of you, you won't just be sharing Mark, but Mark and Millie, his wife. That means that her DNA is going to get in the way of searching for his family (we will address that in just a minute). So if you already have to deal with Millie's DNA, you don't want to have to deal with the DNA of Gabe and his wife. Finding a Best Known Match whose MRCA is the last ancestor you know is the very best route to success.

So what if you can't find that best Best Known Match? No worries. You can work with descendants of Gabe and his wife, but it won't be quite as easy. Read about strategies to find a Best Known Match on page 105. Now, I don't want to get ahead of myself, but you can also try targeted testing (page 224) to make your own Best Match. But we will get into that later.

And, if you are looking for an unknown biological parent, your Best Known Match will be provided for you (yes, like a freebie!). Your Plan will provide you with all the details.

Concept 2: Best Mystery Match
Your Best Mystery Match, or your BMM, which is exactly like your BFF. You know, that person you rely on to help you out when you need something. Your BMM is your best DNA match for whom you don't know

your relationship, but whom you can see is related to the line you want to research.

How can you tell that this BMM is related to the line you want to research? I thought you would never ask! That leads right into our third important concept.

Concept 3: Genetic Networks

A genetic network is a group of people who all connect to you through a common ancestral couple. You likely already understand – but just haven't thought about the concept – that your entire list of DNA matches (no matter how many you have) can be broken up into varying numbers of genetic groups. So, for example, the simplest way to break up your list would be to split it into two groups: one group representing each of your parents. Though actually, in this DNA business, we like to talk about relationships to couples (because it takes two to tango!). So when we

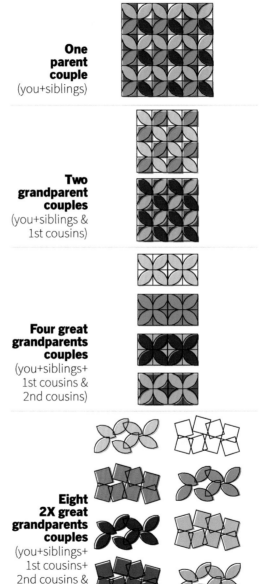

One parent couple
(you+siblings)

Two grandparent couples
(you+siblings & 1st cousins)

Four great grandparents couples
(you+siblings+ 1st cousins & 2nd cousins)

Eight 2X great grandparents couples
(you+siblings+ 1st cousins+ 2nd cousins & 3rd cousins)

split the list in two, it is really representing your two grandparent couples.

Warning: This little system I am describing only works perfectly when your lines are not related to each other. If you know you have individuals in your family tree who married their relatives, then you have to adjust your thinking (see page 190 about pedigree collapse if you just have one or two crossovers, and page 130 regarding endogamy if your family is repeatedly related to itself, and page 187 if you are related to your match through more than one line).

If you move back a generation, to your great grandparents, you can now split your list into four groups, one to represent each great grandparent couple. What would happen if you moved back another generation? Right! You would have 8 groups, one for each set of 2X great grandparents, and, well, you can see where this is going.

Your goal then, is to find the genetic network associated with the line you want to research. Essentially, you want to find the people in your match list who are related to your missing ancestor, and use what they know to help you identify your missing person.

Sometimes you will need to find another genetic network to help you, and your Plan will go over that when it's time. The important thing you understand right now is the reason you are doing this. Identifying and working with more than one network can significantly increase your chances of finding your common ancestor. The strategy is summed up in my Ask The Wife methodology, which you can read about on page 212, or you can just wait until you get to that section of your Plan.

Concept 4: Genealogy Research
The very nature of your genetic network means that your DNA matches within that network should all share some kind of common ancestral connection. To find out who that is (or to confirm others' research), you will have to DO GENEALOGY RESEARCH. That means you are looking through everyone's family trees to find common surnames and locations, and doing more research to try to figure out how they are related. Later

sections in the book will walk you through this process, including steps to take when your match doesn't have a detailed family tree (or any family tree).

Once you are able to see a common ancestor *within* the trees of your matches, you have done it! You have very likely found your family. But in many cases, you will not have the name of your missing ancestor, but instead the name of your ancestor's ancestor.

Sometimes you will have to go back in time: find the ancestors of your match's ancestor, and then come back forward in time to find all of the descendants of those ancestors until you identify your connection. Sometimes you'll just need to go one direction, if solid research has already been done going the other direction (is your head spinning yet, or are you sharpening your pencil?). We will go over all of that in the step-by-step guides in your Plan, but for now, you should just take a deep breath. The genetic part is over. It is all about genealogy from here.

So, how are you feeling? Feeling like you can handle these four concepts (with my help, of course!)? I think you can too. Let's double check. By the end of this section you should be comfortable with the following concepts.

 **Check for understanding before you begin:**

1. To start this process you need a Best Known Match: someone who is related to the ancestor you want to research. Or, if you are looking for a biological parent, all you need is you.

2. If you need to, you will use your Best Known Match to find a Best Mystery Match.

3. Your entire DNA match page can be grouped into a varying number of related groups. To identify an ancestor, you need to find the group(s) in your match list that is related to the ancestor you are looking for. We call this group a genetic network. You will create a genetic network with the help of your Best Mystery Match.

4. You will do genealogical research to find out how members of the group are related to each other. Identifying their common ancestor means you have identified someone who is somehow related to you. We then DO MORE GENEALOGY (and sometimes more genetics!) to figure out how.

choose your research goal

If you just want to know how you are related to a DNA match on your list go to page 40.

For those of you who have a specific ancestor you want to research, use this family tree as if it were your own and find the generation of the ancestor that you want to research. Then turn to the corresponding page in this book for a step-by-step Plan on how to find a name to fill in that blank space.

28

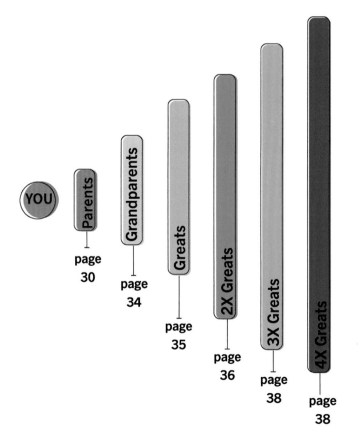

YOU

Parents

page 30

Grandparents

page 34

Greats

page 35

2X Greats

page 36

3X Greats

page 38

4X Greats

page 38

Notice that only ancestors back to your 4X great grandparents are included. If you are trying to go back further than that, autosomal DNA isn't the right tool for you. In fact, it took a lot of hemming and hawing for me to even include 4X greats on this chart. In the end I decided to just so I can tell you this: I am not sure finding an ancestor this far back using autosomal DNA can be done accurately. There is just too much danger of confirmation bias (see page 124). I don't recommend it.

Even if you are looking for 3X greats you are going to run into a lot of difficulty. You can still try to apply the principles in this book, but it is going to be a lot harder to be certain of your conclusions. Certainly if this is the first time you have tried to do something like this, don't start with your 3X greats! Do you have another ancestor you could practice on first?

All right, enough yammering, find the page number you need in the image provided and let's get started.

searching for biological parents

Welcome. Whether you have known all your life or only recently discovered you have a missing biological parent, this is an exciting and turbulent path you are embarking on. Before we start, I just need us to be on the same page about a few things before we move on.

1. Are you really sure you want to know? Because as I said in the introduction to this book, this methodology works. Even if you don't find out today or tomorrow, if you start walking down this path you will find an answer eventually.

2. This decision affects a lot more people than just you in both positive and potentially negative ways.

3. Everyone has a right to know about their biological family. But no one has a right to a relationship. Those are two different things. DNA testing and methodology will give you the knowledge; the relationship part is totally separate (and a lot more complicated).

30

Thanks for reading that. Now: I am excited to help you find out more about you.

Just a heads-up before we get started. Because of the way DNA is inherited, unless you can see a half sibling or a parent on your match list (now or in the future), your DNA match list may take you further down the road to discover your parent(s), but it will likely not be able to take you all the way. What I mean is, your DNA cousins are going to help you identify the family you are from, but without more testing, you likely won't be able to find out exactly who your father or mother is or was. For example, your DNA matches might lead you to a family that had four boys. Without further testing or more information (like, if you learn that only one of them was geographically near your birth mom nine months before you were born, but even that is speculation), you will not know for certain which of the four boys is your father unless you test each boy or one of their known children. I am aware of many situations where two or more boys are candidates, but they are deceased and they had no children. In these cases it is not (currently) possible to confirm the identity of the biological father.

To have a hope of even identifying a smallish pool of people who might be your biological parent, you need to have at least one second cousin in your match list. Or, if you want to be technical, one person sharing more than 90 cM of DNA. If you do not, it will be very difficult and very time consuming to figure out how you are related to your more distant matches. And, as I mentioned, in the end you likely just have a list of names, and no definite answers. Now, the way your Plan is written, I have included possibilities for researching DNA matches who are not as close as second cousins, but it is not a path I recommend. Why? Because the best a third cousin can do is identify one set of your 2X great grandparents. You have 8 sets of 2X great grandparents. Having only one identified means there is still a lot of genealogy to do, and very few clues to tell us when we are on the right track. Still, don't let me stop you if you are determined to see this through, no matter the cards you have been dealt.

If you are looking for your father, it will be very helpful if you have your mother tested. If your mother is unavailable, a half-sibling of yours on your mom's side would be excellent (or really anyone who is related on your mom's side).

Before you jump in with both feet, your ethnicity results may offer excellent clues to the identity of your birth parent(s). However, even if you have a 50/50 split, between Africa and Ireland, that doesn't always mean you have one parent who was African and another who was Irish. They both could have been a mix of both. So be careful. But just having some idea of the heritage of your father or mother might be helpful moving forward. And don't forget to pay attention to those genetic communities (page 13).

OK, let's get started.

 First a question: Are you male or female? If you are a male, and looking for your father, head over to page 232 to learn how your YDNA can help you, then come right back here to keep working with your atDNA test.

The first thing you need to understand when working with atDNA is how we are measuring relationships. We measure relationships in something called a centimorgan. Please take just a few minutes to go read all about those tiny but powerful bits of DNA on page 103.

Go on, go read it, even if you feel like you already know all about them.

All set? Feel like you have a good grasp on what all the fuss is about? Good.

If you are looking for both of your parents, you are ready to start at ground zero of your Plan. **Go to** page 57 to see what you need to do first.

32

If you're looking for just one birth parent, keep reading here.

 Has the other side of your family done any DNA testing? Meaning if you are looking for your father, has your mother been tested – or anyone on your maternal side? Or if you are looking for your mother, has anyone on your father's side tested?

 You are ready to jump into your Plan. **Head over KM.1 on** page 44 **to get started**.

 If not, do you know much about your other parent's genealogy? For example, do you know the names of your grandparents? **If yes, see** page 155, then come back here and move onto the next question. Or, you can skip this part and just treat yourself like you don't know who your mom is and begin at step MM.17 (page 57).

OK, so you have now built a small tree for your other parent's family.

Looking at your match list, can you identify a first or second cousin match that is related to your mom's family?

Great, head over to **KM.1** (page 44).

 No worries, just treat this situation as if you don't know your mom and **begin at step MM.17** (page 57). The Plan will ask you to start research with your Best Mystery Match.

33

Important: If you realize at any point in the process that this Best Mystery Match is related to your known side, stop wherever you are, and take that known match to KM.1 on page 44 and begin this process again.

searching for grandparents

I hope you are ready to find your grandparents, because your chances are very good.

But before we jump in, the first thing you need to understand is how genetic relationships are measured in autosomal DNA testing: with a unit of measure called centimorgans. Please take a few minutes to read all about those tiny but powerful bits of DNA on page 103.

Go on, go read it, even if you feel like you already know all about them.

OK, just one more thing before we get started. If you are looking for a grandparent because you think your parent was adopted or illegitimate, you need to be familiar with half relationships. So head over to page 174 to read all about it, and then come back.

If you are missing both of your grandparents, you are essentially going to be following the same Plan as an adoptee, as it is likely that your parent does not have any siblings that they know of. So **head over to KM.1** on page 44 to label all of the matches on the known side of your family.

If you are only looking for one grandparent and your parent does have a half sibling who has tested (if they haven't get them tested! Or even their child—your half first cousin—get them to test!), **still go over to KM.1**, but after finding and labeling all the matches on your known side, use this known half sibling (or their child) to label all the matches related to the known grandparent. Then proceed as outlined in KM.1.

searching for great grandparents

Congratulations: you have chosen to find an ancestor that is in the absolute sweet spot of genetic genealogy research. For most people, the ancestor you are looking for in this range has passed away, and many were born before 1940, which means when we get to that point, we might actually be able to find what we need to identify them by name in readily available, digitized records. So I hope you are ready to find someone, because your chances are very good.

The first thing you need to understand is how genetic relationships are measured in autosomal DNA testing: with a unit of measure called centimorgans. Please take a few minutes to read all about those tiny but powerful bits of DNA on page 103.

Go on, go read it, even if you feel like you already know all about them.

OK, just one more thing before we get started. If you are looking for a great grandparent because you think your mother or father or grandparent was adopted or illegitimate, you need to be familiar with half relationships. So head over to page 174 to read all about it, and then come back.

All set? Feel like you have a good grasp on what all the fuss is about? Good. Time to get to work. **Turn to KM.11** on page 45 to find your Best Known Match.

searching for
2X great grandparents

While not as easy as identifying a grandparent or great grandparent, using your DNA to identify your 2X great grandparents is still very do-able. When assessing the feasibility of a project like this, it helps to think about what kinds of cousins can help you identify your ancestor. Other descendants of your missing ancestor's other children (not your great grandparent, but one of his/her siblings) are your third cousins, right? (Go ahead, go back and read that again.) The reason that finding an ancestor in this generation is tricky, but still very possible, is the way that inherited DNA behaves in this kind of third cousin relationship. To help me explain, first go to page 103 and read all about the centimorgan, the all-important unit of measure for DNA. Then come back here.

I'll wait.

All done reading?

OK, so as you learned, the centimorgan can be a bit unpredictable in any relationship, but as you start creeping back towards these 2X great grandparents, the variability in your relationships gets even greater. So what does this all mean for you? It just means that you are going to need to be more flexible in your interpretations of the data. Your Plan might talk in concrete steps and absolute relationships, but you need to always be thinking about alternative possible relationships.

Now I don't want to get too far ahead of myself, but I am guessing that even at this point you want a little more information. So let's talk over an example. Let's say in your Plan you find someone you believe to be your third cousin. Let's call him Jim. The problem is, Jim shares 80 cM and at that level of shared DNA there are at least TEN relationships that you could have with Jim. Contrast that to the situation where you and

Jim share any amount of DNA over 100 cM and your top relationships include a much shorter list of possible relationships.

All I am saying is that you are going to need patience and persistence in this process. You may need to go back and try things again with a different relationship in mind.

Aaand (yes, there's more) you need to think about half relationships. Read about those on page 174.

OK, enough nay-saying, time to get to work. **Turn to KM.11** on page 45 to find your Best Known Match.

searching for
3X great grandparents

Are you sure? *Really* sure? I know when you picked up this book you were excited that it might actually help you find this missing ancestor. And it still might. But I want to tell you up front, you are dancing on the edge of what DNA testing can actually do.

When assessing the feasibility of a project like this, it helps to think about what kinds of cousins can help you identify your ancestor. So other descendants of your missing ancestor's other children (not your 2x great grandparent, but one of his/her siblings) would be your fourth cousins, right? Finding an ancestor in this generation is tricky because you only share DNA with half of your true fourth cousins. So even people who are documented descendants of the ancestor you are trying to find may not be able to help you solve this mystery because they may not even show up on your DNA match list. (Read more about sharing DNA beginning on page 103, in the section on centimorgans.)

So what does this all mean for you? First of all, it means you are definitely going to need more than just you to solve this problem. You will need to gather every possible documented descendant of your known ancestor. So head over to page 138 to read all about how to use close relatives in your search, as well as page 224 to start thinking about some targeted testing.

It also means that you are going to need to be more flexible in your interpretations of the data. Your Plan might talk in concrete steps and absolute relationships, but you need to always be thinking about alternative possible relationships.

Example time. Let's say in your Plan you find someone you believe to be your fourth cousin. Let's call her Sarah. The problem is, Sarah shares 45 cM and at that level of shared DNA there are at least TWENTY (yes, that is 20!) relationships that you could have with Sarah. Contrast that to the situation where you and another match named Jim share any amount of DNA over 100 cM and your top relationships tally up to about 5.

All I am saying is that you are going to need patience and persistence in this process. You may need to go back and try things again with a different relationship in mind.

OK, enough ominous warnings. Time to get to work! You *can* do this. You just need to settle in for the long haul. And I hope you like genealogy, because you are going to be doing a lot of it. Probably mostly for other people.

Turn to KM.11 on page 45 to find your Best Known Match.

identifying a DNA
mystery match

So you have a Mystery Match, eh? It might be just a new match on your list, or I have heard from so many of you how you are trying to help an adoptee find out how they fit in your family. This can be a very rewarding exercise, and can help to spread the fun of real genealogy work to other people. But just a word of caution if you are helping someone else: this is THEIR search. They get to decide how much information you go looking for and what to do with the relationship once you figure it out.

First, let's talk centimorgans. Those are the things we use to measure genetic relationships. Please take a few minutes to read all about those tiny but powerful bits of DNA on page 103.

Go on, go read it, even if you feel like you already know all about them.

Now let's start out with some realistic expectations. If your Mystery Match is sharing less than 50 cM, settle in for the long haul. It is going to be tricky to figure out exactly how you are connected because your relationship may be fairly distant. Your success is really dependent on the strength of your match's tree and of your own tree as well as how many DNA matches you have. For tips on building out your own tree before tackling this match, see page 155.

OK, now we are ready to get to work. Make sure you are writing down all of your steps and findings in your research log (page 199).

Before we complicate this with more investigation, use the Shared Matches tool (page 209) on this Mystery Match.

Do you see any mystery matches in this network who share more DNA with you than this match?

Yes OK, then I want you to **switch** your analysis over to this more closely related Mystery Match, who we are going to call your Best Mystery Match. Let's first figure out how you are related to this person, and then you can come back to this match you originally picked out. I need you to **go back and run the Shared Matches tool on this new Mystery Match,** then keep going with the next question. Once you figure out as much as you can about this new Mystery Match, start the process over with your original Mystery Match.

No That's ok. Next question.

? Do you see anyone in that shared matches list that you already know your relationship to?

Yes Fantastic. **Go to KM.54** (page 48) to use the known matches in your network to narrow down your relationship.

No OK, no problem.

? Do you have any half siblings or first cousins who have tested and who show up on your main match page
(but apparently aren't showing up in this shared matches list, because you are answering no to the above question)?

Yes OK, if this Mystery Match is sharing more than 50 cM but is not sharing DNA with your close relative, then you can hypothesize (notice I am NOT saying this is a sure thing) that this Mystery match is not related to you in the same way that these close matches are related. For example, if your paternal first cousin has tested, but doesn't match this Mystery Match, the Mystery Match is likely related on your mom's side. So now you know *something*. But if you want to know more, continue here as if you answered no to the above question (but don't forget what you learned here).

All righty then, let's figure out how you are related to this match.

Does your match have any kind of tree?

Go to MM.3 (page 51) and let's see what we can learn about them. On that page I am going to ask you again if your match has a tree. Just bear with me: answer *Yes*, and keep going. **OR**, if you want to, instead of taking this route, first answer *no* here. Then if you can't find what you are looking for in this route, come back here and head over to MM.3 and keep going.

42

Without a tree for your mystery match, we have to take a purely genetic approach. To do that we are going to employ the Leftovers Strategy on page 222.

Check for understanding: After reading and implementing the Leftovers strategy you should have labeled as many matches in your match list as possible using known DNA matches.

After using the Leftovers strategy, does your Best Mystery Match have a label?

Well, then you have found the branch of the family that your match is related to! From here you would just need to **Do Genealogy** to figure out exactly how you are connected. If you want help figuring out when in your family tree and when in your match's tree you should be looking for a common ancestor, use the Plan starting at **MM.4** (page 53) to help (see note about MM.4 below).

 Well, then you know that this Best Mystery Match is NOT related to any of the lines you have labeled. Which means they may just be able to fill in a hole! So **take this match to MM.4** (page 53), and follow the Plan to see what you can learn.

A note about moving on to MM.4 from here: Since this match doesn't have a tree, unless you have a compelling reason to assume otherwise, just move forward as if your match is *not* removed from you, meaning that you are on the same generation. That statement will make more sense when you get to MM.4.

43

KM.1 Identify and Label Known Matches

Starting with a known match is the fastest way to zero in on your missing ancestor.

In this step you will gather all matches that are related to your known side of the family with the Shared Matches tool, using the process outlined on page 209. **You will use your closest tested known relative as the Best Match**.

The Shared Matches process will give you a list of matches who are related to your known parent's family. Label them (see page 176) so you can separate them out from matches related to your unknown parent or grandparent, and therefore leave them out of your analysis. When labeling matches to look for a parent or grandparent, you will generally only need to label individuals who are sharing 40 or more cMs with you (to find this number, see page 103). You can label more people than that, but when looking for a relationship this close, it usually isn't necessary.

44

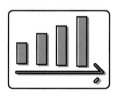

Progress Check

Before moving on, you should have used the Shared Matches tool to identify and label all your matches on your mom's side (if you are looking for someone on your dad's side) or on your dad's side (if you are looking for someone your mom's side).

All good? Great. Now **go to MM.17** page 57 to find your Best Mystery Match.

KM.11 Find a Known Match

Starting with a Best Known Match helps you filter your match list to find the matches who are in the best position to help you answer your question.

Your Best Known Match is someone whose MRCA is the generation *younger than* the ancestor you are looking to find:

So if your missing ancestors are your:

> Grandparents—your Best Known Match would be your sibling.
> Great Grandparents—1st cousins
> 2X greats—2nd Cousins
> 3X greats—3rd cousins
> 4X greats—4th cousins
> For tips on finding your Known Match, see page 105.

45

Were you able to find a Known Match (a match whose MRCA is the ancestor you are looking for)?

No | How about a match whose MRCA is TWO generations younger than the hole in your tree you are trying to fill? An example relationship fitting that description might be (but isn't limited to) your:

> Great Grandparents—sibling
> 2X greats—1st cousin
> 3X greats—2nd cousin
> 4X greats—3rd cousin

If the match is your sibling, they really don't help right this minute (but take a look at page 138 if you have had other close relatives test), so you will actually need to answer *No* to this question (see below). If yes, you have a match in the generation younger than the MRCA, skip down to, well, *YES*.

 Still a no?

No worries. Let's move on to finding your Best Mystery Match in **MM.28** on page 60.

 Fantastic. Write down in your research log (see page 199) an entry for this Best Known Match. List their name, the total amount of DNA you are sharing (for help in finding that number, see page 103), and any other details you find important.

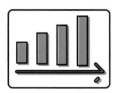

Progress check

Before moving on, you should have found a Best Known Match, and written in your research log all their details.

Now scoot over to **KM.43** on page 47 to check genetics vs genealogy.

KM.43 Check Genetics vs Genealogy

We are going to base much of our future evaluation on the integrity of this Known Match, so we want to make sure they are who they say they are.

Now that you have your Known Match in hand, you need to make sure that the genealogical relationship you see on paper is correctly translating to the genetic match you see in their DNA. We call this checking your genetic vs. genealogical relationship, and you can read about it on page 111.

Check for understanding: After reading about the genetic vs genealogical relationship, you should have learned how to look at the total amount of DNA shared with this Known Match and compare it to your known genealogical relationship to see if the two agree with each other.

And? What do you think?

Do the genetics and the genealogy of this Known Match agree?

Or maybe only sort-of? I would be a little cautious using this match going forward. So you have two choices here:

1. Throw caution to the wind and **just press on to MM.19** on page 58.

2. Find a New Known Match. You can either choose another match you may have seen when finding the first, or if there seems to be a lack of descendants from this person you want to research, you could **try employing the Leftovers strategy** (page 222) to find your Best Mystery Match and **then moving on to MM.3** (page 51).

Wonderful. **Let's keep going to MM.19 on page 58).**

When trying to decide how you are related to a match in your match list, it helps if you can spot some known matches.

Get out a copy of your own family tree that you can write on.

Take a look at the genetic network you just created for this Mystery Match by using the Shared Matches tool. Any match on this list that you know your relationship to is a Known Match.

Choose your most closely related (to you) Known Match.

On your family tree, circle the MRCA (see page 22) between you and this Known Match.

Is this closest Known Match sharing more DNA with you than your Mystery Match?

48

 OK, take a look at your family tree. When your Mystery Match is sharing more DNA with you than your Known Match the common ancestor between you and your Mystery Match is somewhere between the MRCA of your Known Match (where you have circled) and you. If you want more details, jump down to the Next Steps.

Yes | Your Mystery Match is related to an ancestor of the MRCA you share with your Known Match.

Do you have a Known Match in this genetic network who is sharing less

DNA with you than your Mystery Match?

Yes — Circle the MRCA you have with this second Known Match. Now look at the generations in between your first circle and your second circle. Somewhere in there is the connecting ancestor with this Mystery Match. If you want more details, jump down to the next question.

No — Well, you have isolated the line that connects you. If you want to know more about how you are connected, see the next question.

? Does your match have any kind of tree?

Yes — **Go to MM.3** (page 51) and let's see what we can learn about them. On that page I am going to ask you again if your match has a tree, just bear with me, answer Yes, and keep going. Sections MM.3 - MM.5 are going to be teaching you how to find the generation of connection with this Best Mystery Match. If you and/or your match already have ancestors filling those spots where you are supposed to connect, and you don't see common ancestors, then there may be a disconnect between the genetics and genealogy for either you or your match. Just keep working the Plan as if you do not have ancestors in those generations. This will help you keep an open mind and allow the DNA to try to tell you what it can about who does fill those spots.

So, go on, go jump into the Plan at MM.3 (page 51).

No — Using a Known Match, you have already identified a general line that this match is related to. Without a tree for your mystery match, you could just DO GENEALOGY and find out as much as you can about this branch of your tree, and hopefully identify this match in the process. But, it might help to know just a little more about your generation of connection.

Go jump into the Plan at MM.4 (page 53) to try to figure out more details about how this match fits into your tree.

MM.3 Estimate the Age of Your Best Mystery Match

Estimating the age of your Best Mystery Match helps you to center your research around the right generation.

It's time to try to guess the age of your Best Mystery Match, which can often help you decide if they are likely in your generation or if they are a generation (or even two!) older or younger than you are. While this doesn't always work, it can help you figure out your most likely relationship. When you know your most likely relationship, you know where in this match's chart to start looking for your common ancestor. It may seem like an extra step — but trust me, it's a time saver.

 Does this match have any family members listed in their family tree?

No If you have another match who shares a similar amount of DNA and has a family tree posted, it is best to start with that match. But if this match is in Match Block #3, or is just sharing the most DNA by far, then it will be worth it for you to turn to page 141 (about Finding Living People) and use those strategies to try to build a family tree for that person, then come back here and keep going. If you aren't able to find any genealogy for this Best Match, or you just want to get to work without looking for living people (which honestly, can take a while), **you will need to choose a new Best Match** (one that does at least have one other person in their tree) and keep moving.

If you don't have a new Best Match, you can still try to estimate your generation of connection. Just continue on with this plan by assuming that you and your match are on the same generation, meaning that you are not removed. Continue down to the **Progress check** in this step.

 With even a small family tree, you can estimate the age of

your Best Mystery Match, and thereby decide their most likely relationship to you. Look for a birth year for a parent (or parent's sibling) if possible; if not, a grandparent (or grandparent's sibling) or great-grandparent (or sibling). That birth year can help you estimate the age of your match. On average, mothers are about 25-30 years older than their children, and fathers about 30-35 years older. Of course there are instances that fall well outside this range, including birth parents who may not have raised a child because they themselves were quite young. (Read more about how that average age range between generations has been determined at https://isogg.org/wiki/How_long_is_a_generation%3F_Science_provides_an_answer).

Check out page 195 for help in determining not only the age of your match, but also if you are once or twice removed from them.

Go ahead, I will wait here.

Great! You have now determined if your match is removed from you (if you couldn't figure it out, just start out by assuming you are in the same generation, and proceed with the Plan). Make sure to write down your conclusion in your research log.

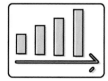

Progress check: Before moving on, you should have:

1. Identified your Best Mystery Match.

2. Written down the total amount of DNA shared with your Best Mystery Match.

3. Determined that your match has at least a small tree posted in their account (or decided that didn't matter).

4. Determined if this Best Mystery Match has a relationship that is removed from you.

Good.

On to MM.4 on page 53.

MM.4 Find Your Most Likely Relationship To Your Best Mystery Match

Using a combination of genetics and genealogy can help you zero in on the most important parts of your match's tree.

OK, now that you have figured out if your Best Mystery Match is removed from you, it's time to estimate your relationship to them, and find the all-important generation of connection: the place in their tree and your tree where you should find your common ancestor (don't jump ahead, I am just letting you know it's coming up in step MM.5).

Start by taking that total amount of shared DNA I had you write down earlier, and head over to page 180 to determine which block your Best Match is in and (by using your knowledge of whether you are removed) what your relationship most likely is to them. Write it down in your research log, then come back here for your next steps.

Disclaimer: must read before continuing! These things we call centimorgans are relatively unpredictable little things. We do have good information on how they work and how they combine to reveal relationships, but they are actually fraught with problems. So before you move on, you MUST read the *Unless* clause on page 227.

Now that you have read the *Unless*, and you have a relationship picked out for your match (and you wrote it in your research log!), you are ready to move on with your search.

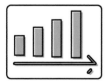

Progress Check: Using the information on page 180, you have identified the Match Block of your Best Mystery match, and you understand all of the variability associated with this method.

If your match is in Match Block 3 — turn to NS.44 on page 96. **Otherwise, go to MM.5** on page 54.

MM.5 Find Your Generation of Connection

Finding the generation of connection will guide much of the genetic and genealogy research we do in later steps, so take your time, and let's figure this out.

All righty, now that you have used your knowledge of the age of your Best Mystery Match and the Match Block to determine your most likely relationship to this Best Mystery Match, let's find your generation of connection. **Head over to** page 147 to figure out which of your match's ancestors are going to fill in which branches in your family tree.

 Check for understanding: You have TWO generations of connection, one in your match's tree, and one in your tree. These may or may not be the same. You must first figure out which ancestor in your match's tree is your ancestor. Then you can figure out where in your tree that new ancestor fits.

54

In your research log, **write down the relationship you see** in the column in the table from page 147 labeled *Your Match's Ancestor*. **This is your generation of connection in your Best Mystery Match's tree**. One of their ancestors in this generation is very likely related to you somehow.

In future steps in the Plan you will see your relationship listed with other possible relationship types that others going through this same step (but for a different ancestor) might be looking at, too. So the step might say something like this:

"You should have already written down the generation of connection in your match's tree as your match's grandparents/great grandparents/2X great grandparents/3X great grandparents/4X great grandparents, right?"

When you see all of the relationships in a line like that, just choose your relationship that you have just identified (and written down!) and read the sentence with just your relationship, ignoring all others.

Quick reminder: If you identified your generation of connection with this match as one or both parents- **go back to** page 57 **in MM.17**. At the bottom of that step you should have redirected to NS.44. **So go back to MM.17** and make sure you have been directed to the right place.

If you are delving into half relationships, be sure to read up on those on page 174 before you continue.

If the ancestor you identified as shared with your Best Mystery Match is more distant than your 4X great grandparents, I am sorry to say, you just won't have much chance of finding your shared ancestor using your DNA. There is just too much genealogy involved, and too much genetic variation at play. Feel free to keep going and learn what you can about your family, as you may be able to find out *something*. I just want you to know that at the end of all of this it is unlikely you will have narrowed your search down to one candidate that could fit the hole in your family tree. your missing ancestor.

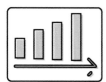

Progress check: Phew! That was a lot. By this point you should have:

1. Used the total amount of DNA you share with your Best Mystery Match to estimate your generation of connection. This means you used the chart on page 147 to figure out which of their ancestors likely appears in your family tree.

2. You have written down that ancestor in your research log.

You will probably be relieved to know that we are going to leave the genetics behind for a minute and do some genealogy!

Yay!

Head over to DG.23 on page 76.

Unless you are arriving here with the goal of identifying a match on your list who does not have a tree. Then, well, this is about as far as the DNA can take you. If you are determined (of course you are!) you can try the techniques on page 141 to help you find living people to see if you can figure out a little more about this person. If you are able to use that resource to figure out more about this match, start over in this Plan with that new information and try it again.

MM.17 Identify Your Best Mystery Match (Unknown Parentage)

Your Best Mystery Match is the key to your research.

Take a look at the top of your main match page, and identify your Best Mystery Match. **That's the one at the top of the list with no label.** We will refer to this person as your Best Mystery Match.

Write down in your research log (page 199) an entry for this Best Mystery Match. List their username, the total amount of DNA you are sharing (for help in finding that number, see page 103), and any other details you find important.

Using that total amount of DNA number, take a quick peek at the chart on page 180 (don't read the text yet, just look at the table) to see if this Best Mystery Match is in match block one or two. If so, turn to NS.44, **on page 96.** If not, onward, my friend, to **Step MM.3** (page 51).

MM.19

Your Best Mystery Match is the key to your research.

Using the Best Known Match you just identified, use the Shared Matches tool to create a genetic network surrounding this match, as outlined on page 209. Label these matches with the surnames of the ancestral couple you share in common with your Best Known match, as suggested on page 176.

Find the match in this genetic network who shares the most DNA with you, but for whom you do not know your relationship. This person will be your Best Mystery Match.

Remember, when you used Shared Matches you found people related to the ancestral *couple* that you share in common. So when you are choosing your Best Mystery Match, you are trying to avoid matches that you think might be related to the ancestor you are NOT looking for, right? This match should share less DNA with you than your Best Known Match.

58

Why should this match share less DNA? People who share more DNA than this Best Known Match should be related to you more closely than your Best Known Match and therefore do not share your target ancestor as your MRCA, but a closer relative. For example, if your Best Known match is a second cousin because you are researching your great grandparent, using Shared Matches on this Best Known Match is going to find your first cousins who are also related to this line. We don't want to use those first cousins in this next step since their MRCA is not your great grandparent, but a generation sooner, in your grandparent.

Do you see the match I am talking about?

If you used the Shared Matches tool on your Best Known match and you don't see ANY shared matches, well, you've got trouble. There are two good reasons for this outcome:

1. Your Best Known match is a 4th cousin. If you are at AncestryDNA, when you use the Shared Matches tool, you will only see individuals on the list who are 4th cousins or closer to BOTH you and your Best Known Match. So, it is possible that you just don't have any matches that meet that criteria.

2. There just aren't any matches to be found. This might be because your ancestor was an immigrant (and left behind all close relatives in another homeland where today people aren't commonly taking DNA tests), or for some reason their line did not produce any descendants who have taken a DNA test.

59

Whichever the case, you may be feeling a bit frustrated. What to do: You might try some targeted testing (page 224). Or maybe search your match page by surname or location to find other people who have the surname and location you are researching in your family tree (page 201). Ultimately, you may need to **head over to Getting Unstuck** for some ideas about where to go from here (page 171).

Wunderbar! Time to find out more about this Mystery Match. **Head to MM.3 on** page 51.

When you aren't adopted but you still can't find a Best Known Match, you need a new way to find a Best Mystery Match.

You find a Best Mystery Match using the one of two strategies:

A. If you know most of your other ancestors, try the Leftovers strategy on page 222.

B. If you have lots of holes in your family tree, try the Cousin Category strategy on page 219.

Both strategies might take you a little while, so I am going to get started on this crochet project I have been itching to try. I will be back.

Done?

 Do you have your Best Mystery Match in hand?

 Still can't find that Best Mystery Match? You may need to talk to an expert. Check out our DNA Mentoring options at www.yourDNAguide.com/mentor.

 Take your Best Mystery Match to MM.3 (page 51). A little later on in the Plan you will be using the Shared Matches Tool on this match. If you are coming from the Counting Cousins strategy, you may have already done this. That's ok. Just do it again, and move on.

MM.76 Find the Spot in YOUR Chart Where Your Best Mystery Match's Ancestor Fits

With the names of a new ancestral couple in hand, you need to figure out where that couple fits in your tree.

Before we can talk about how the relationship of your Best Mystery Match and your Best Tree Match affects you, you need to add one more piece of information to this puzzle. **You need to find out which ancestor on YOUR chart this genetic network is going to help you fill in**.

This might get a tad confusing, so plan to read this more than once. It always helps me to read it out loud (in fact, I am even talking out loud as I write it). Up until this point we have been talking only about your Best Mystery Match's pedigree chart and finding which of your Best Mystery Match's ancestors is your ancestor. You should have already written down the generation of connection in your match's tree as your match's grandparents/great grandparents/2X great grandparents/3X great grandparents/4X great grandparents, right?

OK, that is in THEIR tree. But what about YOUR tree?

If you determined that you and your match are on the same generation, then this is easy-peasy. Their grandparents/great grandparents/2X great grandparents/3X great grandparents/4X great grandparents are the same as your missing grandparents/great grandparents/2X great grandparents/3X great grandparents/4X great grandparents.

But if you and your match are removed at all, it can get a little dicey. That's why I made the handy chart on page 147. So head over there, and find your relationship to your Best Mystery Match in the first column. Then look at the last column to see the spot on YOUR pedigree chart where this identified ancestor belongs.

Find it? Great!

Write it down.

Then go to DG.64 on page 80.

GN.8 Shared Matches Tool

The Shared Matches tool should be the tool you are using every day—10 times a day—in your genetic genealogy research.

By determining that the generation of connection is in the grandparents/ great grandparents/2X great grandparents/3X great grandparents/4X great grandparents of your Best Mystery Match, and finding all 4 of the grandparents/8 of the great grandparents/16 of the 2X great grandparents/32 of the 3X great grandparents/64 of the 4X great great grandparents for your match, you have now likely brought to the surface the ancestor or ancestral couple that connects you and your Best Mystery Match. All you have to do is figure out which of those ancestor(s) you just identified are your shared ancestor(s).

This may be as simple as asking your DNA match list for more information. To do that, you will **use the Shared Matches tool**. So head over to page 209 and when the instructions ask for a Best Match, you are going to be using this Best Mystery Match we have been working with.

I am going to grab one of my husband's homemade croissants (yes, he bakes!) while I wait.

Check for Understanding: After reading all about shared matches you should have learned that:

1. The Shared Matches tool is a filter that helps you find the matches you need to focus on.

2. When you use Shared Matches on this Best Mystery Match, you will be collecting other people who are related to this Best Mystery Match in some way.

3. Unless they aren't related. For the reasons mentioned, we have to be careful when using shared matches.

All righty, so you have used the Shared Matches tool on your Best Mystery Match and now you have a nice tidy group of matches to work with.

And viola! Just like that, you now have the basics of a **genetic network**. Somewhere among these matches and their genealogy is the answer to your question. If you haven't already, be sure and label these matches as part of this network so you can easily find them later. Read all about labeling on page 176.

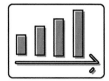

Progress Check:
By the end of this step you should have:

1. Used the Shared Matches tool on your Best Mystery Match.

2. Labeled these shared matches with the name of this Best Match (or any other name you have decided on).

Now, let's keep moving with The Plan so you can find your ancestor! If you are in this to find an ancestor, your **next stop is DG.14,** page 73.

64

GN.22 Find a New Mystery Match

Remember that your entire match page can be divided into groups, but eventually those groups converge in a couple who (hopefully) married. That's who you are looking for.

After reading the section on the Ask The Wife strategy you should understand that in order to find out which descendant of an identified ancestral couple is your ancestor, you need to find DNA evidence of a connection to the spouse of one of the children. That DNA evidence comes in the form of another genetic network.

The first step to create this new genetic network is to find a New Mystery Match. **Someone who is not related to your Best Mystery Match or to any of your other known lines of your family**.

There are two ways to find this New Mystery Match, and it depends on how you found your Best Mystery Match.

If you found your Best Mystery Match by just selecting your top match, either because you were adopted or because you used the *Leftovers* strategy (page 222), finding your New Mystery match is pretty straightforward. **Just look back at your match list and choose the next best match that doesn't have a label**. That person likely represents a different genetic network in your tree, which is exactly what we are looking for.

If you found your Mystery Match **using a Known Match**, go back to the genetic network you initially created with your Known Match and **choose the top match that does not yet carry the label** of your initial Best Mystery Match.

WARNING: Remember, if you used a Known Match to create your genetic network, the people you have gathered represent the ancestral *couple* you share with your Best Known Match. So this new match you find might be related to your target ancestor OR that ancestor's spouse. Likewise, if you used the Leftover strategy, then this new match could represent any line in your family tree that you were not able to label - so again, it might be for this target line, and it may not. So just keep that in mind as we move forward.

 Do you have a New Mystery Match identified?

 Good job. **Move on to GN.47** (page 67).

No You may want to try the Leftovers strategy (if you haven't already) outlined on page 222, then continue on with the Plan from here.

 Did that work? Did using the Leftovers strategy help you find your New Mystery Match?

66

No Still no? **Try going back** to your initial genetic network created by your Best Known Match and expanding that network using the information on page 133. Then look for a New Mystery Match.

By expanding the network, were you able to find a match that shares DNA with your initial genetic network, but is not sharing DNA with your Best Mystery Match?

 No? Sheesh. OK, **looks like you might be stuck**. Head over to page 171 to try to get unstuck.

GN.47 Find a Genetic Network for your New Match

You've got this. Let's find a genetic network for this New Match.

Starting in MM.19 (page 58), you are going to create another genetic network centered around this New Mystery Match. This means you will go all the way through the Plan again until you find the common ancestor for this new genetic network. That will likely be in DG.14 or GN.51. Go for it. Keep in mind that the Plan will continue to say Best Mystery Match, but just know that you will be working with your New Mystery Match.

I know it's going to take you a while, so I am going to go help out at my son's middle school volleyball practice. I'll be back soon.

Are you back? Me too. Phew! There is such a difference between 6th grade boys and 8th grade boys, don't you agree?

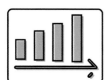

OK, progress check:
You have a brand new genetic network, headed up by your New Mystery Match. You have found a New Common Ancestor (that's what we are going to call this ancestor you found that connects your new genetic network together).

 Can you see a connection between the tree of your New Common Ancestor and the tree of the ancestor you found with your Best Mystery Match?

 Turn to page 94 (**NS.37**) for help when Ask Wife fails.

Yes Wow. Way to go, you. **Go to NS.65** on page 97 for your next steps.

GN.51 Expanding Your Genetic Network

The more people you can find who are genetically related to the line you are researching, the better chance you have of finding two people within that group who share a connection to each other.

If you are having trouble finding related ancestors in your genetic network, you may need a bigger network. Head over to page 133 to read all about expanding your network (responsibly). Remember, once you find more people to add to your network, you may have to go back to MM.3 (page 51) to find their generation of connection and then do their genealogy back to that generation so you can see your shared ancestor.

It is a bit misleading that there is only this one measly line between the above paragraph and the next question. But don't be fooled, this is not a simple thing I have asked you to do. It will take lots of time. Just whenever you finish, come back here.

68

Did it work? By expanding your genetic network and doing other people's genealogy, were you able to see a common ancestor between the people in your group?

Still no? Ugh. It **looks like you might be stuck**. Head over to page 171 for help. If this isn't your first time through this process and you are working a New Mystery match, you can certainly try the getting unstuck strategies. But if they don't work, head back to GN.22 (page 65) and find a new Best Match.

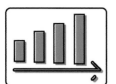 Nice work! The match you found that shares an ancestor with your Best Mystery Match is going to be called your Best Tree Match. It's totally ok if you have more than one (in fact, the more the merrier!)

 Progress check: By now you should have:

1. Identified a genetic network, or a group of people who are all sharing DNA.

2. Found a common ancestor or ancestral couple between at least two members of your genetic network.

All done? Great, **let's move on to** page 61, **MM.76**.

DG.10 Find More Tree Matches

The more people you can find who connect to the tree of your Best Mystery Match, the more certain you can be of your own connection to these matches.

This, my friend, is the fun part. You know, the *genealogy* part. Well, it is part genealogy and part private eye. You need to start with the matches in your genetic network that share the most DNA with you, but for whom you don't have a pedigree that extends all the way back to your generation of connection. So use the resources on page 163 (Quick and Simple Tree) and page 141 (Finding Living People) to help you find more genealogy connections to your Best Mystery Match and Best Tree Match's common ancestor so you can be sure we are working with the right people. Remember that part of staying organized is that as you find them you add these matches to the family tree you have created for your Best Mystery Match (see page 168).

When you find these matches and add them to the tree, be sure to **check their genetic vs genealogical relationships** (page 111) against where you think you might connect in this tree you are making. If you have more than three or four matches who seem to share a common ancestor, checking their genetics and genealogy is best achieved by drawing out their relationships in the What Are The Odds Tool (see page 168).

70

? Were you able to find a few more matches who are descendants of the MRCA ancestors for your Best Mystery Match and your Best Tree match?

No You can try expanding your genetic network on page 133, using this Best Tree Match you have found to help. Or, you can still move on, but just be careful and realize that the ancestral couple you have identified might not be your connecting couple. But you may connect in the generation closer or more distant than them.

 Fantastic. Another question for you:

 Did the genetics and the genealogy check out? Meaning the WATO tree agrees with your placement on the tree? Or you checked the genetic and genealogy relationships with the members of your network manually and it all looks good.

 Mmmm... looks like you might be stuck. Head over to page 171.

 Still yes? Great!

 Let's check in: At this point, you should have the name of a shiny new ancestor in your hand. The ancestor that you identified is shared by your Best Mystery Match, and your Best Tree Match, and any other tree matches you have found in your genetic network.

Does this ancestor (or ancestral couple) fill the most recent hole in your genealogy that you were looking to fill?

Yes Then **congratulations**, you are an official genetic genealogist! You found your ancestral couple, the parents of your ancestor (and you thought he was deposited by aliens!). Now it's time to tell your story. For help see page 226.

No This ancestral couple you identified must be more distant than your missing person. What I mean is that there is still a gap in your tree between the ancestor you know and the shared ancestor you have identified.

Let's go fill that gap: **move onto DG.33** (page 78) to identify your ancestor in the next generation.

72

DG.14 Find the Genealogical Connection Between Matches in Your Genetic Network

Since you don't know the name of the ancestor you are looking for, you have to figure out how your matches are related to each other, which will then lead you to your answer.

Let's review what you have accomplished so far:

1. You have identified the generation of connection for your Best Mystery Match. That means that you have a list of your match's grandparents/great grandparents/2X great grandparents/3X great grandparents/4X great grandparents, and you know that one of those couples or one of those ancestors is also your family. (Not sounding familiar? Go back to MM.3 on page 51.)

2. You have identified and labeled a Genetic Network: a group of people who are very likely related to this Best Mystery Match and one of their grandparents/great grandparents/2X great grandparents/3X great grandparents/4X great grandparents somehow. (Didn't quite finish that? Go back to GN.8 on page 63.)

Next goal: Find out how the matches in this genetic network are related to each other. Remember from page 209 about shared matches that all these people don't necessarily all share one common ancestor, but we are hoping that most of them do.

Why? Because if you can see that multiple DNA matches have a connection to a particular ancestral couple, then you know that you are somehow related to that couple and you can focus your research on this particular line in your match's family tree.

Try this first: The Quick Scan

Using the list of surnames you created when you were drawing on your match's tree (page 128), do a quick scan through the family trees of the matches in your genetic network, looking for any common surnames with this list. Remember that you can often expand the family trees of these matches by making a Quick and Simple Tree as we talked about on page 163.

Unlinked trees (at AncestryDNA) can be helpful, but be careful. An unlinked tree means that there is a tree in your match's account, but they haven't gone through the extra step of linking their DNA sample to their tree. So it is possible that they are the home person in the tree, but then again, they may not be. But that doesn't mean that the trees aren't valuable. On the contrary, they could contain just the information you need. If you do decide to use what you find, make a note in your research log that the information came from an unlinked tree. Even DNA matches who have linked trees could have other unlinked trees in their account that may hold valuable information. Click on the name of your match to see all the public trees in their account.

? Were you able to see a single shared common ancestral couple between any matches in your genetic network and your Best Match?

Notice I said *single* shared. Don't stop looking after you have found one, just in case there is another — that will make a big difference as we move forward.

No That's ok, we have more tricks up our sleeves. If you want to take a **genealogy approach,** turn to **section DG.88** on page 83 and learn how to do other people's genealogy.
If you would rather take a **genetic approach** (but don't worry, you will end up doing plenty of genealogy), **head over to GN.51** on page 68 to expand your genetic network.

Yes Woot woot! Way to go you! Say hello to your family! This DNA match you found that has a shared ancestor with your Best Mystery Match will now be known as your Best Tree Match. If you have more than one, even better: they are all Best Tree Matches. Before you build on this success, I want to make sure you understand what a MRCA is. So please read the definition on page 235 before moving forward.

Got it?

OK, if this is your first time through this process, time to **head over to MM.76** on page 61 to find out more about how this identified ancestor fits into your tree. If this isn't your first time and you are dealing with a New Mystery Match and a New Genetic Network, **head back to GN.47** on page 67 and pick up where you left off.

75

DG.23 Extend the Genealogy of your Best Mystery Match

We need to be able to see enough of your Best Mystery Match's tree to make our work productive.

To set yourself up for success in this analysis, you will need this Best Mystery Match to have a family tree that extends back to this generation of connection you just identified.

? Does your match have both grandparent couples/all four great grandparent couples/all eight 2X great grandparent couples/all 16 3X great grandparent couples/all 32 4X great grandparent couples listed in their family tree?

No Turn to page 163 (Building a Quick and Simple Tree) to help you find all the ancestors you need to get started. Don't spend gobs of time on this. Perhaps set the timer for 20 minutes and scout around to see what you can find, using the tools on the page I just suggested. Then move on with the genetic analysis as laid out below. If you get stuck later, you may want to come back to this step and be more thorough with this pedigree creation. Remember, your goal is to find as many surnames and locations that are associated with this Best Mystery Match as possible. This will help you later when you are trying to figure out how this person is related to other matches.

 (You lucky dog!) Fantastic, let's record some things in your research log. With the tree of this Best Mystery Match in hand, we want to take some notes on it. **Head**

over to page 128 **to draw on your match's tree, then come on back here**.

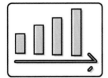 **Progress check:** OK, by now you should have in hand (and recorded in your research log):

1. The name of your Best Known Match (if you had one)

2. The name of your Best Mystery Match

3. The total amount of DNA you share with this Best Mystery Match

4. Your estimated relationship to your Best Mystery Match

5. The generation of connection you share in this Best Mystery Match's family tree

77

6. Notes on your Best Mystery Match's tree to set yourself up for success in later steps

Great job. This is a good place to stop if you need a snack, or a nap (I could use both!).

Whenever you are ready, let's **move ahead to step GN.8** (page 63) in the Plan, unless you are following the Plan to simply **identify a Mystery Match, then turn to DG.14 (page 73).**

Sometimes your Best Mystery Match will connect to you in a generation or two beyond your hole, leaving a gap that needs to be filled.

You have found an ancestor or ancestral couple that likely belongs in your tree. However, this isn't the ancestor you were looking for. It is the ancestor of your ancestor, right?

So let's stop and think about what this really means. In the table below, find the generation of connection you share with your Best Mystery Match as identified in MM.76. Next to that is something simple, but profound: the relationship that this ancestral couple's children would have to you. So essentially, by identifying the common ancestor you share with your Best Mystery Match, you have uncovered a multiple choice question: **Which of the children of this couple is my ancestor?** (Unless this couple only had one child, and then, well, you are set!)

78

Your generation of connection with your Best Mystery Match	Their child would be one of your...
great grandparent couple	4 grandparents
2X great grandparent couple	8 great grandparents
3X great grandparent couple	16 2X great grandparents
4X great grandparent couple	32 3X great grandparents

Assuming they had more than one child, you have some more work to do. I think it will help if we go through an example. Let's say that your shared ancestral couple with your Best Mystery Match is William and Charlene. They had 5 children. One of their children is your grandparent/ great grandparent/2X great grandparent.

But which one?

As long as you can assume that this child of theirs married and had a child that is your ancestor (as opposed to having a child without leaving something as helpful as a marriage record), we can use more fun genetic genealogy techniques to find them. I call this strategy Ask The Wife, and you can read about it on page 212.

Go on—go read it. I will wait here.

 Check for understanding: After reading the Ask The Wife section you should understand that your next step is to find another genetic network that is related to the genetic network associated with your initial Best Mystery Match.

Head over to GN.22 (page 65) to help you implement the Ask The Wife strategy and lead you to the right child of your identified great grandparents/2X great grandparents/3X great grandparents/4X great grandparents.

DG.64 Evaluate The Relationship Between Your Best Match and Best Tree Match

Knowing how these two matches are related to each other helps you understand where their common ancestor fits in your tree.

OK, now we are going to evaluate the relationship between your Best Mystery Match and your Best Tree Match. This will help you figure out your next steps for discovering which of your Best Mystery Match's ancestors are your ancestors. If you have more than one Tree Match, use your match with the highest shared cMs. **Please read through the information below as you take a look at the graphic on the next page.** This image, and the text below, helps you find out what your next step should be based on the relationship of your Best Mystery Match and your Tree Match.

In the image, the first column is asking you about the relationship between YOUR generation of connection with your Best Mystery Match, and the MRCA generation between your Best Mystery Match and your Tree Match. Wait—what did I just say? Let's try that again, using a step-by-step.

1. Look at your research log where you have the tree of your Best Mystery Match. You should have a box around your generation of connection. If you don't, go back to page 128 and add one, and then come back here.

2. On that tree, circle the MRCA ancestor that your Best Tree Match and your Best Mystery Match have in common.

3. Now look at the relationship between the box (which represents your generation of connection with your Best Mystery Match) and the circle on the tree and decide if the circle is before the box, on the same generation as the box, or after the box.

4. Take this information into the first column of the chart below

and follow the instructions, depending on the scenario you have.

In the ASK section of this chart, I am asking for some specifics about your generation of connection to your Best Mystery Match. If that spot is in your great grandparents or closer, we get to move on much faster without as much double-checking. So, find where you are in the image to find your next steps, and get going!

Here's a quick reference for the page numbers you need, depending on where you end up needing to go:

NS.5.1 page 84

NS5.2 page 85

NS5.3 page 86

NS5.4 page 87

NS5.5 page 89

NS5.6 page 91

Next Steps

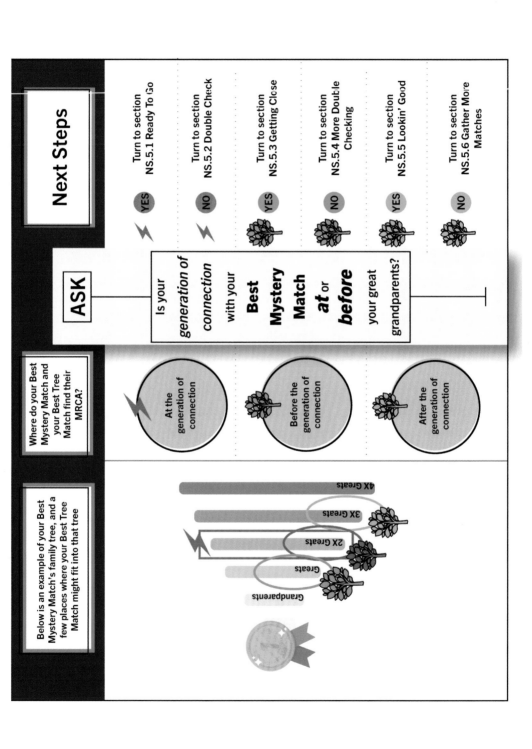

Below is an example of your Best Mystery Match's family tree, and a few places where your Best Tree Match might fit into that tree

Grandparents
Greats
2X Greats
3X Greats
4X Greats

Where do your Best Mystery Match and your Best Tree Match find their MRCA?

At the generation of connection

Before the generation of connection

After the generation of connection

ASK

Is your *generation of connection* with your **Best Mystery Match** *at* or *before* your great grandparents?

YES — Turn to section NS.5.1 Ready To Go

NO — Turn to section NS.5.2 Double Check

YES — Turn to section NS.5.3 Getting Close

NO — Turn to section NS.5.4 More Double Checking

YES — Turn to section NS.5.5 Lookin' Good

NO — Turn to section NS.5.6 Gather More Matches

DG.88 Do Other People's Genealogy

Taking your match's small tree into a larger tree can be surprisingly satisfying, and often very fruitful.

If you have looked through your genetic network and you aren't able to see a common ancestor between members of your group, it might just be because your matches haven't posted enough genealogy. Remember, to see a common ancestor, you will have to take your match's genealogy all the way back to your generation of connection. So far, we have only figured out the generation of connection for your Best Mystery Match. So **a good strategy is to take your New Best Match** (or the match in your genetic network who is sharing the second-most DNA with you after your Best Mystery Match) **and make sure their family tree** (if they have one) **is pushed out all the way to the generation of connection**.

To find that generation for this new match, head back to section MM.3 page 51) and use this match to work yourself back down to step DG.14 (page 73).

Does this sound like a lot of work? It is. But the minute you see that shared ancestor between two of your matches, it actually does make it all worth it. I promise.

Changed your mind? Rather take the genetic route? Go for it. **Start on page 68 with GN.51** and expand your genetic network. But be forewarned, you will still need to do other people's genealogy before this is all said and done.

This is the simplest option (take a minute to thank your ancestors and your DNA matches).

The spot we are filling in YOUR tree (remember you figured this out in MM.76) with your Best Mystery Match's ancestor is either your grandparents or great grandparents, and your Best Mystery Match and your Best Tree Match have their MRCA in the generation of connection we determined for your Best Mystery Match. That means you can now say with cautious confidence, "Hello, Family!" That's right: the ancestor or ancestral couple you found shared between your Best Mystery Match and your Best Tree Match is also your grandparents (if that was your connecting couple) or great grandparents, assuming your matches' tree research is correct.

Got it?

If you have found your grandparents, **you may just want to DO GENEALOGY**, as one of their children should be your parent. At this point, without any closer matches, you are as far as DNA can take you. **The rest is up to you. See NS.44** (page 96).

If it is your great grandparents you have found, you are probably ready to **move on to DG.33** on page 78 to figure out which of their descendants is your ancestor. But if you want to be extra sure before you move on (it can't hurt, right?) **I suggest working through section DG.10** on page 70 first, as finding more matches that connect to this family will just make you feel more confident moving forward.

NS.5.2 Let's Double Check

According to what you learned in MM.76 and the fact you are on this step, the ancestor your match is helping you fill in is either your 2X great grandparents/3X great grandparents/4X great grandparents. Your Best Mystery Match and your Best Tree Match have their MRCA at this very same generation of connection. This means that the couple you see as their shared ancestral couple likely fits in your tree in that same generation. So, again, depending on your generation of connection, you have just found your 2X great grandparents/3X great grandparents/4X great grandparents.

Maybe.

You need to add an extra layer of analysis to be sure you have found your common ancestor. This is because the amount of shared DNA with these kinds of matches can just get a little wonky and can lead you astray if you are not careful.

You really need more information to be sure. So try one of these strategies (or both!) so you can be a little more certain of your relationship to this Best Mystery Match and Tree Match before we move on.

> 1. Find more Tree Matches (**DG.10 on page 70**).
>
> 2. **Expand your genetic network** using the resources on page 133. Once you do that, **move on to step DG.10** on page 70.

OK, so if the ancestor your Best Match is helping you fill in (according to MM.76) is your grandparents or great grandparents, and your Best Match and your Tree Match have their MRCA in a generation *younger than* the generation where you connect, then their shared ancestor is either your aunt/uncle (if you connect at grandparents), or a great aunt/uncle (if you connect at the great grandparents. Check out your next steps, depending on which it is:

NS.5.3.1 Your match's MRCA is your aunt/uncle. **That means you need to DO GENEALOGY** to find all of the siblings of this person, knowing that one of them is your parent. If their MRCA is a couple, you will need to do the genealogy for both people, as you don't know which one you are related to. At this point, without any closer matches, you are as far as DNA can take you. **The rest is up to you.** Find your next steps in NS.44 on page 96.

NS.5.3.2 Your match's MRCA is your great aunt/uncle (or in other words, their ancestor's sibling is your grandparent).

Maybe. Maybe your ancestor is their sibling. Let's double check.

Ok, **off with you to DG.10** (page 70)! Find more Tree Matches!

NS.5.4 More Double Checking

Since the ancestor your Best Mystery Match is helping you fill in is further back than your great grandparents, you need to add an extra layer of analysis to be sure that you have found your common ancestor. This is because the amount of shared DNA with these kinds of matches can just get a little wonky and can lead you astray if you are not careful.

According to what you learned in MM.76 and the fact you are on this step, the ancestor your Best Mystery Match is helping you fill in is either your 2X great grandparents/3X great grandparents/ 4X great grandparents. Your Best Mystery Match and your Best Tree Match have their MRCA at a generation before you connect with your Best Mystery Match. This means that one of the people in their shared ancestral couple is a child of your 2X great grandparents/3X great grandparents/4X great grandparents. So that means that your ancestor is a sibling of one of the people in this identified MRCA between your Tree Match and your Best Mystery Match. Feeling like you need a picture to be able to process that one? Me too. Try this.

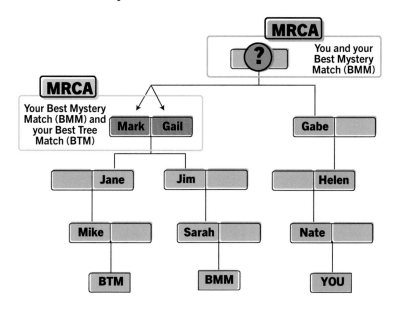

In the image you can see that your Best Tree Match and your Best Mystery Match connect at Mark and Gail. But DNA tells us that you connect with your BMM one generation above that. Which means your ancestral couple is either Mark's parents OR Gail's parents. Which makes your ancestor Gabe either Mark's brother or Gail's brother.

Hopefully it now makes more sense that your ancestor is a sibling of the MRCA of your Best Mystery Match and the Tree Match.

Maybe. Maybe your ancestor is their sibling.

We have to put the *maybe* in there because of the amount of DNA you are sharing. You really need more information to be sure. So try one of these strategies (or both!) to be a little more certain of your relationship to this Best Match and Tree Match before we move on.

1. Find more Tree Matches on page 70, DG.10.

2. Expand your genetic network on page 133. Once you do that, move on to step DG.10 page 70.

NS.5.5 Lookin' Good

OK, the ancestor your Best Mystery Match is helping you fill in is your grandparents or great grandparents (according to MM.76). Your Best Mystery Match and your Best Tree Match have their MRCA in the generation *after* you connect with your Best Mystery Match. That means their shared ancestral couple is one of your great grandparent couples (if you are looking for your grandparents), or one of your 2X great grandparent couples (if you are looking for your greats).

If your Best Tree Match and your Best Mystery match connect in a generation more distant, you will need to adjust these relationships accordingly.

This information is very helpful as it tells you which of your Best Mystery Match's ancestors is your shared ancestor (hint: the one who is a descendant of this Best Match/Tree Match MRCA couple). See the picture here if you like that sorta thing.

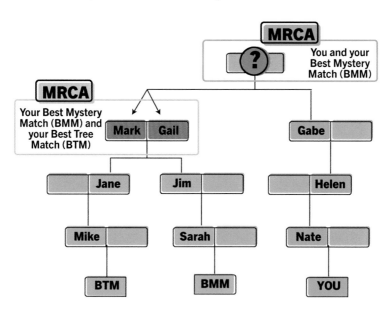

In the image you can see that your Best Tree Match and your Best Mystery Match share a common ancestor in Mark and Gail. DNA says that you and your Best Mystery match should share a common ancestor the generation before this.

And just like that, you have figured out which of your Best Mystery Match's ancestors is also your ancestor. If you have found your grandparents, **you may just want to DO GENEALOGY**, as one of their children should be your parent. At this point, without any closer matches, you are as far as DNA can take you. The rest is up to you. You have two main choices:

1. Wait for a new match to test. You would want a half sibling or half niece or nephew to test.

2. Write a note. See page 117 for some tips on contacting close matches.

3. I know I said only two, but there are three: Just be satisfied you have found your family.

90

If it is your great grandparents you have found, **you are probably ready to move on to DG.33** on page 78 to figure out which of their descendants is your ancestor. But if you want to be extra sure before you move on (it can't hurt, right?) **I suggest working through section DG.10** on page 70 first, if you haven't already.

NS.5.6 Time to Gather

Since the ancestor your match is helping you fill in is further back than your great grandparents, you need to add an extra layer of analysis to be sure that we have found your common ancestor. This is because the amount of shared DNA with these kinds of matches can just get a little wonky and can lead you astray if you are not careful.

According to what you learned in MM.76 and the fact you are on this step, the ancestor your Best Mystery Match is helping you fill in is either your 2X great grandparents/3X great grandparents/ 4X great grandparents. Your Best Mystery Match and your Best Tree Match have their MRCA at a generation *after* you connect with your Best Mystery Match. This connection should help you see which of your Best Match's ancestors is your shared ancestor (hint: the one who is a descendant of this Best Match/Tree Match MRCA couple). The image on this page shows a closer connection than you have, but the idea is the same.

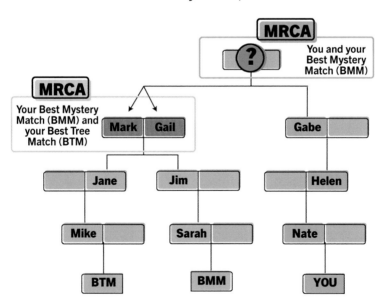

In the image you can see that your Best Tree Match and your Best Mystery Match share a common ancestor in Mark and Gail. DNA says that you and your Best Mystery match should share a common ancestor the generation before this.

Maybe.

We have to put the *maybe* in there because of the amount of DNA you are sharing. You really need more information to be sure. So try one of these strategies (or both!) to be a little more certain of your relationship to this Best Match and Tree Match before we move on.

1. Find more Tree Matches on page 70 DG.10.

2. Expand your genetic network on page 133. Once you do that, move on to step DG.10 page 70.

NS.8 The Answer

It feels good to get this far, doesn't it?

The reality is, without a closer genetic match, it will be difficult to positively identify a closer relative, even if all of the genealogy clues line up. If you are able to do the DNA and the genealogy to find possible parent candidates, you cannot be certain you have found the right person without further DNA testing. At that point you will have two options moving forward.

1. Be satisfied that you have found your family.

2. Delve into the realm of records for living people (page 141) and try to identify their children or grandchildren who would be your potential relatives.

3. Contact the potential parent, or the children of the potential parent to ask for help in solving your mystery. See page 117. This help may come in the form of information they have about your parent, or in their willingness to take a DNA test. See page 224 for more information.

Well, you have come a long way, and hopefully picked up most of the answers you were looking for. Sometimes you have to just be patient until more information is made available to help you find more complete answers to your questions. New matches are coming into your DNA match list every day, so be patient, and diligent, and likely if you haven't found them already, your answers will be forthcoming in the near future.

Great job getting this far.

Time to celebrate. Then **head over to** page 226 for some ideas on how to tell this story.

If you can't see how your two networks fit together, it is probably because they don't.

OK, so you found a New Mystery Match, you built a genetic network around that match, and you were able to find a common ancestral couple within this new match group. Remember that we are calling this ancestor your *New Common Ancestor*. However, you aren't able to see a genealogical connection between the New Common Ancestor and the common ancestor you found with your first genetic network — the one created by your Best Mystery Match.

The most likely explanation for this is that this New Common Ancestor represents a separate line on your family tree, and is not related to your Best Match Common Ancestor.

Here's what I mean: If your Best Mystery Match's Common Ancestral couple (or ancestor, if you are half, which I am not going to be listing, but you need to be thinking) fills one of the two great grandparent couples/ four 2X great grandparent couples/eight 3X great grandparent couples/sixteen 3X great grandparent couples missing in your tree, then this unrelated network may just fill in a different hole.

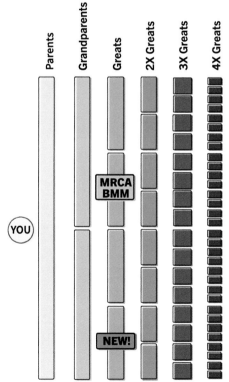

In the image you can see that the MRCA with my Best Mystery Match (BMM) fills my paternal grandfather's mother's line, while my New genetic network corresponds to my maternal grandmother's mother's line.

So the best thing to do is set this genetic network and its New Common Ancestor aside, and start back at GN.22 (page 64), and **make a *New* New Genetic Network** using a New Best Mystery Match.

If you do that, and you still can't see connections between any of your genetic networks, you may be stuck. See page 171 to help you get unstuck.

NS.44 A Close Relationship

When you share this much DNA, your relationship is relatively easy to define, and the ancestor you are seeking is within reach.

If you are sharing enough DNA with your match that you have landed in match blocks one, two or three, congratulations, your genetic genealogy journey has already found you an answer. To be seeking in this generation range you must be looking for a biological parent. Looking at the match block where your Best Mystery Match is found you have identified is likely your:

Match Block #1: Parent or Child

Match Block #2: Full Sibling

Match Block #3: Half sibling, Aunt or Uncle, Niece or Nephew.

If you are in Match Block #3, you should have already decided which of these relationships applies to you and your match in MM.4 (page 53) when you determined if your match was removed from you, and you reviewed the table on page 180.

So what now? What should you do now that you have found this close relative? Well, before you move forward, **it is essential that you read Discovering Close Family Relationships - Things To Consider** on page 126.

OK, now that you are hopefully thinking clearly, let's discuss your choices for next steps, there are a few:

1. Contact them. See page 117 for tips on contacting these Close Matches.

2. Do genealogy. If you are in Match Block 2 or 3, you could do genealogy to find out more about your parent(s) on your own. For tips on researching living people, see page 141.

3. Be satisfied with what you have already found. Perhaps it is enough.

Now that you have reached this point in your journey, there is only one thing left to do. **Tell your story.** For some ideas, see page 226.

NS.65 Two Genetic Networks in the Books

Finding two genetic networks that meet in an ancestral couple might just be one of the best feelings you will ever have when doing genetic genealogy.

Was your generation of connection with your Best Mystery Match your great grandparents?

Congratulations! By identifying how two genetic networks connect, you just found your grandparents. If you need to keep going, you must be looking for your parent. That means that from here, you may be getting into the realm of living people. So you can **move on to NS.8 on page 93** to find out some next steps.

OK, so that means that the ancestral couple you identified when you found the connection between two genetic networks was more distant. When looking at the ancestral couple you just found, think about your original research goal, and ask yourself the following question:

Was this the hole you were trying to fill?

Wonderful! Way to go, you! Feel free to do the happy dance (I suggest the Charleston). Then head over to page 226 to tell your story.

You still need to come a generation further to find your missing ancestor?

OK, by now maybe you can guess what I am going to say: get to work! You can take the genetic route or the genealogical route. Start again.

1.   Genealogy route: **Do genealogy research** (surprise!). You could just find all of the children/grandchildren/great grandchildren of this couple (however far you need to come down) you just discovered, and find out which one was in the right place at the right time to be your relative.

2. Go back to GN.47 on page 67 to **find a New New Mystery Match**.

learning guides

automated clustering tools

We spend a lot of time in this book and in genetic genealogy in general taking long lists of people and parsing them out into smaller groups that we hope have some kind of relationship to each other. We call it making a genetic network, but you could also call it clustering.

It doesn't take anyone very long to realize what a terribly tedious process this is, and to also recognize that much of what we are doing by hand (figuring out which of our matches are related to each other and how) can be automated.

When the first automated clustering tool was released I was SO EXCITED. Even though I knew it meant less job security for me, since if a machine could do what I do better and faster than I can, I would become obsolete.

Well, I am still here.

I am still here not because these tools aren't great and not because the tools don't work. They do.

Mostly.

However, these tools and their very pretty pictures still require a fair amount of interpretation. You still actually have to understand everything I am teaching you in this book to really understand what the autocluster tool is telling you.

I have found that actually going through the process of making a genetic network by hand helps me to understand exactly how the thing was created, and therefore approximately where it should fit in my tree.

But I can see why you might find the automated clustering tools useful.

So here's what I am recommending: Try my method of doing it the old fashioned way for the creation of *at least one* genetic network. Then if you want to use automated clustering tools to cluster your entire match list, be my guest! I hope when you use them you will have a better understanding of what to do next.

All of the tools produce an image much like the one below from Genetic Affairs. The tool at its core is just a matrix. The program clusters all of the matches who share with each other, creating groups of matches according to parameters that you can set.

One of the big problems with these tools is that every time you get a new match, the autocluster report becomes outdated. So if you are using them often, they need to be updated often.

Accessing automated clustering tools

MyHeritage

If you have transferred your DNA to MyHeritage from another company and paid the $29 fee, or if you tested with MyHeritage directly and have a subscription to their service, you can access the AutoClusters tool right within their site. Go to DNA > DNA Tools > AutoClusters. This tool is the Genetic Affairs tool. See below for more information.

For all other companies your top three choices are:

Genetic Affairs

www.geneticaffairs.com

Free to try, then under $10 for most needs. You provide Genetic Affairs with your login to the testing company and they will group your matches into clusters of related people. The output is both a graphical representation of your clusters as a matrix (shown here in the image) as well as an interactive list of the matches within the clusters that is hyperlinked to the person profile pages

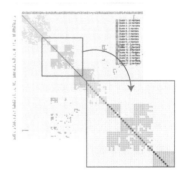

at your company.

Collins' Leeds Method

www.dnagedcom.com

Requires the DNAGedcom Client (www.dnagedcom.com), which has several tools and is $50/year. The output is very similar to that of Genetic Affairs, with an interactive chart and spreadsheet.

Connected DNA

www.connectedDNA.com

See the website for current pricing, but the price does reflect the hands-on nature of this service as it is handled by genetic genealogist Shelly Crawford. She provides several interactive outputs to help you view your clusters in a variety of ways. Below you see two different representations of the same data (pretty, aren't they?). Both are interactive.

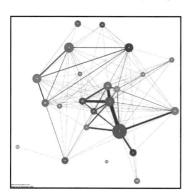 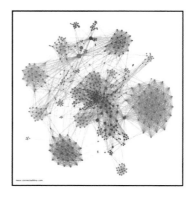

centimorgans:
what you need to know

The amount of DNA you share with someone else is measured in something called a centimorgan (cM). While it is temping to think of a cM like a centimeter, isn't even close to being so simple. It is actually more like a crystal ball, trying to determine how likely it is that you are related to someone else. Very simply stated: the more you share, the more you should care. Meaning: the more DNA you share, the more closely related you are to someone else.

Our DNA testing companies use this number to help determine your relationship to your match, which they report as a relationship range. So you might see a 2nd-3rd cousin who shares 134 cM.

Below are details on how to access this cM information at each of your companies, so take just a minute to check that out before you move on, as we will be using these numbers all the time.

You will learn more about how centimorgans work in the Match Block section on page 180.

AncestryDNA
With AncestryDNA, next to each person in your match list, you will see a summary of your genetic relationship range (like 1st-2nd cousin) and how much DNA you share (maybe 837 cM across 35 segments). Click on the little gray icon with an "i" in it. That will bring up a companion chart showing your possible genealogical relationships to this match, as well as the likelihood of each statistically. Keep in mind that for more distant relationships there will be lots and lots of relationships that are all about the same likelihood. You will see in your Plan how we use this chart in combination with the Match Blocks that will be introduced to you in a little bit.

Family Tree DNA

On the main match page for your Family Tree DNA Family Finder results, you will see a genetic relationship range reported in the third column on your match list, followed by the total amount of shared cMs and the size of the biggest piece of shared DNA in the fourth and fifth columns.

It is very important that you understand how Family Tree DNA is reporting the shared amount of DNA. They are an all-inclusive kind of place. That means they are reporting nearly every tiny piece of DNA they see shared, which actually means that most of the shared cM numbers you see at FTDNA will be higher than they should be, which could really throw off your analysis. So be careful.

23andMe

At 23andMe, you can see the percentage of shared DNA from the main DNA Relatives home page. Click on that match to see a detail view, which you can expand to see an estimated relationship (and other suggested relationships); a corresponding tree diagram; the total shared DNA in cM; and even a chromosome browser view showing where on your chromosomes you overlap with this match.

MyHeritageDNA

On the MyHeritage website, the total amount of shared DNA, total number of shared segments AND even the size of the largest segment is shown on the main match page under the title Match Quality. Click on the question mark icon next to estimated relationships and you'll see a diagram of your possible relationships.

Living DNA

Known as the test that gives you the most British Isles-specific ethnicity reports, Living DNA is still working on its DNA matches experience. At this point, it reports just total shared DNA and a simple predicted relationship.

cheating tools

Starting your search with the right tools just sets you up for success. When fishing for your ancestor, the right tool is the bait. The right bait catches the right matches. The right matches give you the information you need to break down brick walls.

The bait is your Best Known Match. Your Best Known Match is someone else who has a *documented* connection to the line you are looking for. A Best Known Match is someone who is also a descendant of the ancestor you are trying to research. Most often, this person will be related to an ancestral couple in your family tree. So, if you are looking for the parents of Sarah Mitchell, your MRCA (Most Recent Common Ancestor) will likely be a descendant of Sarah and her husband John Rhodes. Ideally, your Best Known Match will be a descendant of a different child of John and Sarah.

You may already have Best Known Matches in your match list right now. Cheating tools are tools provided by our companies with the intention of helping us make faster connections between our genetics and our genealogy. However, just like cheating in other arenas, while it may get you ahead faster, there could be some negative consequences. So please carefully read what these tools are all about and what they can, and can't do, so you will be prepared for the consequences should you choose to accept their hints.

And just to clarify: just because I call them *cheats* doesn't mean you shouldn't use them. They're shortcuts. It's not unethical to use them. In fact, they're lovely and I use them all the time.

Most often we use cheating tools to help us quickly find descendants of ancestors we are trying to research. But these tools can sometimes also provide hits to ancestors we have not yet discovered. These are theories that you can try to prove using a combination of genetics and genealogy (and this book, of course!).

Theory of Family Relativity

MyHeritage's Theory of Family Relativity (TOFR) is a premium tool, available to MyHeritage subscribers, as well as to those who upload their DNA to the site for free and then pay a $29 fee for the DNA tools.

TOFR is basically a giant hinting system that proposes theories of how you might be related to your match. It takes into account data from your tree, your DNA match's tree (if there is one) and any other tree data on MyHeritage (including FamilySearch Tree and Geni.com tree data that is imported regularly), as well as historical records.

> An example theory might go something like this: The theory starts with you (the tester) and connects to a tree at Geni.com, then goes back a few generations and uses a Canadian census record to splice the Geni.com tree to the FamilySearch Tree, then comes back forward in time, back to Geni.com and thence to the DNA match. MyHeritage calls this a "tree traverse system," since it may thread you through several different trees to connect you to your match.

As it says right in the name of the tool, **these are *theories***, and MyHeritage expects you to confirm the possible trees yourself. They're only accurate insofar as the various trees and records are accurate and actually belong to your ancestors. But MyHeritage makes it easy for you to check their work. They put these little green circles above the theory. Those are all points of connection between one source and the next. Those are *clickable*. **The idea is that you'll verify each connection yourself**.

You won't have theories available for every match, but for some, the system may suggest several. "The number of theories you may get depends on several factors, such as the size and level of detail in your family tree (the more the better)," MyHeritage explained in its press release when the company launched the tool. "This number will increase over time as more users test their DNA on MyHeritage or upload their

DNA result, and as we continue to add more historical records and as family trees continue to grow."

If you don't have a MyHeritage subscription (or haven't paid the $29 unlock fee for free upload customers), you'll still see theories the site has proposed for you. But when you click to view the full theory, you won't be able to see all the information.

To explore your theories, log in to MyHeritage and go to your DNA match list. You'll see clickable notations next to those matches for whom theories have been generated. Review the theories carefully, remembering that theories are built off tree and record data alone, and **don't take into account your genetic relationship** (other than the fact that you are a DNA match). MyHeritage recommends that you "compare the relationship suggested by the theory to the relationship suggested by the DNA to see if they are compatible." (See page 111 on genetics vs. genealogy.)

107 Find an article (with a nice illustration of tree traversing) on the TOFR at www.yourdnaguide.com/myheritage.

ThruLines

A similar, but more powerful tree reconstruction tool is the ThruLines feature at Ancestry, available to anyone who has taken a test there. Instead of making you view each match individually like in MyHeritage's TOFR, ThruLines allows you to choose a specific ancestor for whom a ThruLine is available, and see your DNA matches who are that ancestor's descendants. The real power in the tool is that your match doesn't have to have that ancestor listed on his tree. The site searches both public and private-but-searchable trees on Ancestry for genealogy connections between your tree and the one posted by your DNA match. It also consults historical records on the site. Then **ThruLines draws trees to illustrate possible genealogical paths that connect you, filling in any missing holes**.

To explore the ThruLines tool:

1. Log in to Ancestry.com. From the DNA dropdown menu, choose ThruLines or choose the ThruLines box from your DNA home page.

2. You'll be shown a list of ancestors (or potential common ancestors) for whom ThruLines are available.

3. Click on an ancestor's name to explore ThruLine tree reconstructions showing your DNA matches as fellow descendants.

Several matches may appear in your reconstructed tree, depending on how many matches have tested in a particular branch of your family. Ancestors who are already present in your tree appear in solid boxes. Dropdown menus let you view the matches that descend through each branch of the family. Potential common ancestors (suggested by tree connections) appear in dotted-line boxes.

If you click on an ancestor (or even just hover your mouse over the ancestor) it will tell you how many matches you have connected to that ancestor. For your grandparents and great grandparents, you may not have that many. But as you go back in time, most people who have heritage in the United States will have several, if not dozens of DNA matches. If you go back to your 2X great grandfather and you don't see any matches but yourself, this is worth investigating. **It may be a red flag.** Unless you can see documented evidence that this ancestor did not leave many descendants, your DNA might be telling you there is a disconnect between your genetics and your genealogy. Or, it could mean that everything is perfectly fine and your family is off doing other things and they just haven't been tested. But you need to check.

To participate in ThruLines, AncestryDNA customers need to link their DNA results to a public or private searchable family tree; learn how at www.yourdnaguide.com/ancestrydna. Your matches need to do the same. Preferably, your trees will have at least 3-4 generations. Make sure you've added whatever details you can about dates, places and family relationships, not just for direct ancestors but for those siblings, aunts, uncles and cousins who may become those "missing links" in your ThruLines experience.

What I like about ThruLines is the powerful visualization you get for better understanding your overall tree. When you start working on any particular family line, check to see whether ThruLines shows you any DNA matches who share that descent. This is also a great way to see who has tested before your big family reunion (or, on the contrary, which branch doesn't seem to have any DNA matches yet). Plus, it is a great way to find essential Known DNA Matches (page 105).

Remember that the tree reconstruction you see is only as good as the tree data. That's worth restating: **these trees are not DNA based!** They are based only on the genealogical data in trees. You need to verify the tree data yourself. For example, ThruLines suggested that my mom is a descendant of her adopted father, based solely on her DNA match with me, her daughter.

Read an article about ThruLines, with plenty of nice screenshots, at www.yourdnaguide.com/ancestrydna.

23andMe's Family Tree

23andMe has an enormous pool of people who have tested there, so a lot of genealogy connections happen on this site. However, tools for exploring and theorizing family tree relationships here have been slower to come than at Ancestry and MyHeritage. Good news, they now have a Family Tree reconstruction tool that **uses your shared DNA** (not your tree data like the previous two companies) **to visually reassemble a genetic family tree** with your DNA matches on it. This is especially great news for those who don't know their family trees or haven't entered the information into a tree file yet.

23andMe's Family Tree predicts genealogical relationships based on the DNA you share with your matches. It can build a bigger and better tree if you have more matches and if you participate in the site's DNA Relatives tool. It's an interactive tree to which customers may add names of relatives or ancestors.

This is my kind of chart. Simple and beautiful, but also instructive. This is just the kind of thinking and mapping process we have to use to visualize our connections to DNA matches based on our total shared centimorgans, but 23andme is trying to do it for you.

In the Family Tree image you can clearly see the two branches of your tree in different colors, blue for dad and pink for mom (classic!). While it takes a few minutes (ok, maybe longer than that) to figure out exactly what the picture is portraying, relying on your knowledge of how families are organized can help. For example, everyone has two parents and four grandparents (two couples). But if we march back in my tree, we should encounter four great grandparent couples.

Keep in mind while you are looking at this tree that 23andMe doesn't follow the traditional genealogist's format of placing the male on the left and the female on the right. So don't let that throw you. A couple can be listed in any order.

Even though there aren't any names, you can clearly see which relatives of yours (and of your matches) should be connecting you. Assuming the site gets the tree right (and if you don't know any better, it's a good theory to start from), all you have to do now is the genealogy research to identify the unknown links in between. (See page 161 on genealogy research.)

Read an article about 23andMe's Family Tree (again, with pretty screenshots) at www.yourdnaguide.com/23andme.

check genetics vs. genealogy

Your shared DNA with your Best Matches (both Known and Mystery) is used to search the DNA database to find other people who are related to your shared ancestral couple and to help determine your missing ancestors. For example, if your MRCA with your Best Known Match is (or you believe it is) John and Sarah Rhodes, then the DNA you share with your Best Match will be the DNA you both received from that couple. **Before we use these Best Known Matches to help solidify your connection** to Sarah and John or to find other matches who are descendants of Sarah and John, **you want to make very sure that you and your Best Known Matches have the genetic relationship we would expect given your genealogical relationship**. In other words, you'll check your genetics against your genealogy.

As discussed on page 103, relationships in DNA are all based on centimorgans, which is just a unit of measure for DNA. While you are going to use these numbers to try to determine your genealogical relationships to others, it is very important to keep in mind that DNA is completely randomly inherited. That means that it is actually unpredictable. So you have to be flexible in relationship assessments based on DNA. Below are some tips that apply to checking the genetics and genealogy of any kind of match, so I am going to use the generic Best Match here, and I know that you know that I mean any match you have for whom you want to verify the genetics vs genealogy.

1. To begin, the first thing you will want to do is just double check the quality of the genealogical documentation of your Best Match that connects him to your common ancestor. Just take a quick look at your match's tree. Do they have some actual genealogy documents backing up their connections at each generation?

2. Next, determine what your genealogical relationship *should* be to your first Best Match. If you used a Cheat to find your Best Known Match (page 105), that tool will tell you your hypothesized genealogical relationship. If you are arriving at this step after already determining your relationship using the Match Blocks, then you are set as well. If not, you will need to determine it. If you need help, see page 195.

3. Find the total amount of shared DNA between you and this Best Match. All of the companies show you the total amount of DNA that you share with each match, measured in these centimorgans. See page 103 for the section on centimorgans and how to find them.

4. Find the likelihood that the amount of shared DNA corresponds to your known relationship. If you are at AncestryDNA, you can click on the little "i" next to the amount, and it will pull up a table of relationships and likelihoods. Find your genealogical relationship in the table, and note the corresponding likelihood. So, if one Best Match is your second cousin (the MRCA is their great grandparents and your great grandparents), find where it says *second cousin* on the chart and look to the left to find the percentage likelihood. If you are not at AncestryDNA, you will need to use the Shared cM Project tool hosted on the DNA Painter website (www.DNApainter.com, and see page 168) to find your likelihood.

5. In general, as long as the likelihood is not zero, you are probably ok. But because DNA inheritance is so random, it is always a bit dangerous to use the DNA connection between only two people to make or break a relationship. So make sure you are checking this information for all of your Best Matches who connect to this couple. If you find that you have several Best Matches whose shared centimorgan counts are either too low or too high, you may want to reevaluate your connection to your shared ancestral couple, and make sure that you are not missing something about your relationship before you use this match to move on in your Plan.

Now that you have verified your connection to your Best Match, you are ready to put it to work to help you find your ancestor.

Turn back to your Plan for further instructions.

113

chromosome browsers

Chromosome browsers allow you to see the actual pieces of DNA you are sharing with your match. You may have noticed that we haven't talked much about chromosome browsers in this book, and that is on purpose. **Chromosome browsers can be helpful and interesting, but I just don't think they need to be a central part of your strategy.** However, they do help if you want to check segment size, as we discussed on page 204.

You can also use the chromosome browsers at FTDNA and MyHeritage to see how many of your matching DNA segments are over the 10 cM threshold. Essentially, if you are having trouble finding a common ancestor with someone sharing say, 88 cM, take a look at the chromosome browser to see how much of that DNA is really over 10 cM. I have a good example about my grandma in the endogamy resource (page 130) that will help you see how knowing the segment sizes of all of your shared pieces might impact your research.

While each company's chromosome browser looks a little different, there are some common elements.

- Each company lets you add a specific number of matches to the chromosome browser to compare with you (and at 23andMe you can compare other matches to each other, which is a pretty nifty feature).

- Each person who is added gets their own line for each chromosome. So, if you add 5 people into the chromosome browser, there will be five lines under each chromosome number.

- All the gray represents places where no one is matching you.

- Each added match gets their own box at the top of the page and their own color.

- That color is used to show the locations on the chromosomes where you are sharing DNA

- Most of the time the segment is half-identical.

half-identical

This will make you think a little more scientifically than most of you would like to so feel free to skip this explanation. Still with me? Great, science is fun, isn't' it? If you will recall you have two sets of each chromosome: one you got from mom and one from dad. So when you share DNA with a match, you are usually only sharing one of those chromosomes. Thus the term half-identical. This can actually help you spot full siblings, as full siblings are pretty much the only relationship to have fully identical regions of DNA. Though there are other, um, more complicated relationships that also have fully identical regions. Too much information? Maybe, but I know some of you were wondering.

If your Plan calls for it (which it does rarely), here's how to access Chromosome Browsers at each company where they are available (no chromosome browser at AncestryDNA or LivingDNA).

Chromosome Browsing at 23andMe

There are two ways to access the chromosome browser at 23andMe.

1. From the top navigation menu click on *Family and Friends* and then on *Advanced DNA Comparison*.

2. After you click on a match, click on *More DNA Details* under the *Your genetic relationship* section, then click on *Compare with more relatives*.

Either way, this will bring up the actual chromosome browser tool.

On the left you will see you have automatically been added to the first slot under *Compare*. (If you don't want to compare people against yourself, you can hover over your name and then click on the "X" that appears to remove yourself.) You can then choose up to five individuals from the right to compare against yourself. Only your matches who have agreed to share this level of information with you will show up on this list.

Then just click the *Compare* button, and shebang! There it is! You can then hover over each colored piece to see the length and exact location (if you are into that kind of thing) of that shared piece.

Chromosome Browsing at Family Tree DNA

There are three ways to access the chromosome browser at FTDNA.

1. From the home page under the *Family Finder Menu*.

2. In the top Navigation go to myDNA > Family Finder > Chromosome Browser

3. From the Family Finder match page, click on the box beside up to 8 DNA matches, then click on *Chromosome Browser* at the top of the match page.

If you are accessing the page from option one or two, you will need to then add matches to the browser by clicking on the box beside their name, then click *Compare Relationship*.

Chromosome Browsing at MyHeritageDNA

Note: The chromosome browser tool at MyHeritage is a Premium feature and can only be accessed by those who have purchased a MyHeritage DNA test by subscribing to the MyHeritage record collection, or if you transferred to MyHeritage, by paying the unlock fee.

Access the chromosome browser at MyHeritage DNA by going to DNA > DNA Tools > Chromosome Browser. Alternatively, you can see the individual chromosome browser comparison for you and any match by clicking on any match, and then scrolling down to the chromosome browser section.

communicating with your matches

Inevitably, at some point in this DNA journey, you are going to have to put pen to paper (ok, actually fingers to keys) and write a note. Everywhere but Family Tree DNA this will be through the company's email brokering system (at FTDNA you can see your match's email address and send a note directly).

I want you to think of this note like a first date. You heard me right, a first date, minus all the awkward moments. While it may have been quite some time since you yourself explored those turbulent waters, let's go over a few simple rules:

First rule: Address the correspondence with their username on the testing website. Many people administer multiple accounts, so you also need to tell them upfront whose test you are talking about. For example, let's say your DNA match has a username of RosyGold and is administered by username CJRod. You'll address a note to CJRod and reference yourself as a DNA match of RosyGold.

Second rule: Don't talk about yourself too much. Honestly, you are great and all, and your story is important, but what you really want is *their* story, so you need to get them talking.

Third rule: Ask simple, direct questions. Remember that most of your matches don't have much genealogy experience, so keeping your questions fairly general will help.

Fourth rule: Give them an easy action item. Remember our goal: get them to write back. So if you end your note with something like, "Even if you don't know the answers to my questions, it would be great to hear from you, just so I know my note wasn't lost in cyberspace." You might be surprised at how often people will respond to that.

Outlined below are some sample letters you may want to write to particular relatives. This is just something to get you started, and will almost certainly require customization to your own experience. But if you follow the formula, you will likely find yourself with a second date— meaning, a positive response to your first email.

Potential Parent

If you have arrived here, it is because your Plan has helped you find a biological parent. The decision to reach out to a potential parent should not be taken lightly. Perhaps you got all caught up in the excitement of the chase and you are thrilled that you were actually able to solve this big DNA puzzle. Please take a few days to consider your options and talk with trusted friends or relatives about next steps before you reach out. In this situation there are no standards to follow. So follow the Golden Rule (just do unto others as you would have them do unto you). That is the best we can do.

If you have a half sibling or aunt or uncle, or the parent themselves whose DNA test helped you figure this out (which means we are as genetically sure as we can be about the identity of your parent), feel free to use the text below to reach out. If you don't have a close relative to confirm your parent's identity, you need to tread very carefully. Remember the Unless clause (page 227) I made you read! You don't want to reach out to the wrong person. If your unknown parent has not DNA tested, skip down to the next section.

If your birth parent is a DNA match, write them a note using this template:

> Dear (insert your close match's name or username here),
> It is good to meet you here at (name of testing company). I have been really amazed at the things I have been able to find out with my DNA.
>
> Maybe amazed isn't even the word you would use to describe your experience after you finish reading my note. In fact, I am guessing your reaction will be closer to shock.

Our relationship at the DNA testing company says "parent/child."

I know I was pretty amazed to see this (or some other single line about your reaction).

I know you will likely need a bit of time to process all of this information, but if you wouldn't mind just sending me a quick note to let me know that you have read this email and you are thinking about your next steps, that would help a lot. Or hey, even if you just don't feel like you have room in your life right now to deal with this, that's ok, too. Please just let me know if that is the case, and perhaps after some time has passed, I can follow up with you and we can see where we are then.

Thank you for your reply,
Your Name

If your parent has not DNA tested and you are reaching out to them another way, here are some tips:

- Try to reach out to them in a private way where none of their other family members will know without being told. For example, instead of calling or sending a letter to their home, you may consider sending it to their place of work.

- While I am sure you are going to do (or have done) a fair amount of internet stalking about this person, try not to mention any of this to them when you call. It tends to make people feel uncomfortable when they know you have been stalking them a bit.

- What kind of communication is best is really up to you. Again, when trying to minimize other relatives finding out, you don't know if your parent shares an email or social media account with their spouse, so be careful about electronic communication.

Close Relatives (out to first cousins)

So you are fairly certain you know how you are related to this close DNA match, but it is very likely that they have no idea how they are related to you (they need this book, right?!). So it isn't a good idea to spring this kind of news on them right away. While we always, always want to be honest, remember that the goal of this communication is not to schedule regular Sunday dinners or swap family stories. Your one goal in this first exchange is to get them to write back. To do that, you need to make them feel comfortable. Now I know that being honest and making someone feel comfortable don't always go together in this situation but you have to try.

> Dear (insert your close match's name or username here),
> It is good to meet you here at (name of testing company). I have been really amazed at the things I have been able to find out with my DNA.
>
> Maybe amazed isn't even the word you would use to describe your experience after you finish reading my note. In fact, I am guessing your reaction will be closer to shock.
>
> You see, I have been doing quite a bit of research about how DNA testing works and from our DNA test results I can see that we are closely related, and I have been working to figure out how.

OPTIONAL: If you want to just lay it all out there, try this: In fact, I believe that you might be my (half brother/sister, aunt/uncle, niece/nephew). I believe my mother was [enter your mother's location at that time if you know it]. Perhaps your relative [enter here the relationship you believe this person has to your biological parent, like uncle or grandfather] was in a similar location. I know you will likely need a bit of time to process all of this information, but...

> If you wouldn't mind just sending me a quick note to let me know that you have read this email and you are thinking about working with me to figure out our relationship, that would help a lot. Or hey,

even if you just don't feel like you have room in your life right now to deal with this, that's ok, too. Please just let me know if that is the case, and perhaps after some time has passed, I can follow up with you and we can see where we are then.

Thank you for your reply,
Your Name

2nd-5th cousins

When you start talking to cousins in this range, most of them are not going to immediately know the information we are seeking. Most people do not know their great grandparents. You can still ask them about surnames and locations that you believe to be of interest, but honestly, there isn't much chance they are going to recognize them.

Your best strategy here is to get out of your match the information you need to DO GENEALOGY to get back to the information you want. So, here is an example note to a 2nd-5th cousin:

Dear name or username,
It is good to meet you here at (name of testing company). I have been really amazed at the things I have been able to find out with my DNA. I am currently working on figuring out a few things about my (grandfather, great grandmother, whoever it is you are researching). The great news is, I think you can help.

You actually don't even have to know anything about genealogy or DNA to help me. All I really need is to know whatever you do know about your family. Any names or places of your parents or grandparents would help.

I am specifically looking for [insert surnames and locations you are interested in]. But even if you haven't heard of any of those, can you send me what you do know about your parents and grandparents, and I can figure out the rest?

You can even start an online tree pretty quickly if you want to do it that way.*

Even if you don't have time to send me anything right now, please just reply and let me know you received my note.

Best,
Your Name

*You can send them a link to these free tutorials to show them how to add a tree (I'm all about making your life easier):

23andMe:
www.yourdnaguide.com/ydgblog/2019/10/16/link-family-tree-23andme

AncestryDNA:
www.yourdnaguide.com/add-pedigreean

Family Tree DNA:
www.yourdnaguide.com/ydgblog/2020/1/14/family-tree-dna-add-family-tree

MyHeritage DNA:
www.yourdnaguide.com/link-myheritage-dna-test-family-tree

When you send a correspondence to a match, make sure you write it down in your research log as well as make a note at the actual company of the date you sent the note. This will prevent you from duplicating your efforts, and help you plan when to send that second or third note (probably once a month is sufficient).

No Email Response

You have written to your DNA match. Twice. But no response. What now?

First of all, it can be really difficult to tell if your match has read your note. So you don't even know if they know about you yet. It can be very hard to wait, but initially that is usually the best course of action. At most companies you have no way of knowing if your match has even logged in recently.

At Ancestry you can check to see how recently your match has logged in:

1. Click on a match in your match list to bring up their DNA match profile page.

2. Click on their name again, or the name of the person who administers their account.

3. In the box on the left, Ancestry tells you their last signed in date.

Now, just because they signed in recently does not mean they actually saw your message. But, if they haven't signed in recently, you can be pretty certain that they have NOT seen your message.

If you feel you have waited long enough for a response, or you can see that your match has not logged in recently, then you have to decide if you want to try to contact them another way. Contacting them outside of the testing company will require quite a bit of detective work. If you do find them and contact them, it might feel a little uncomfortable for your match, to know that you were snooping around the internet looking for them.

If you are going to go for it, find some tips for effectively stalking someone on the internet on page 141.

confirmation bias

Confirmation bias is basically just good old fashioned favoritism, maybe mingled with a little bit of pride. It's where you think your idea is the best explanation for the situation. You are unable to view every piece of evidence objectively, because you are always trying to prove your point.

This is a very unscientific way to approach any situation. Ideally, you take every new piece of information and objectively try to figure out how it might add to your knowledge of the situation: to either support your position, or detract from it.

Confirmation bias can easily rear its ugly head in your genealogy research, and especially in genetic genealogy. Let's take a very simple example: You believe that Andre is your 2X great grandfather. In your DNA match list you see three people who are descendants of Andre, and you say BAM! Case closed, I was right, my ancestor is Andre.

That is confirmation bias because you haven't checked and double checked all possibilities.

Take, for example, that the three people who match are actually Elsa and her two kids. According to what you have learned (or you still can learn on page 138) about family groups, Elsa's kids don't count! That means you are down to one match with a descendant of Andre.

Did you check your genetic and genealogical relationship with Elsa (page 111)? Did you check her pedigree chart to see if there were other ancestors that you might have in common?

Did you create a genetic network using Elsa as your Best Match (page 209) to see if you could gather more evidence?

Did you ask yourself if there could be other explanations for your shared DNA? Perhaps endogamy (page 130) or multiple relationships (page

187)? Essentially, have you spent some time thinking of how you could try to disprove that Andre is your ancestor?

All the things I have just listed constitute part of "reasonably exhaustive research," which genealogy standards of scholarship say must be accomplished before you can put Andre into your family tree with any certainty.

In addition to following the genealogy standards, a good way to prevent confirmation bias is to talk to a friend. A good friend. The kind that isn't afraid to tell you that you have food between your teeth. Ask her (or him) to try to poke holes in your theory (and then offer to listen to one of their genealogy stories, just to say thank you). Often an outside perspective is enough to shake you out of your bias, and put you on a path that will ultimately lead to a more confident—and likely more correct—conclusion.

125

discovering close family relationships
things to consider

You have connected with your biological parent or sibling or uncle and you are both likely experiencing a roller coaster of emotions. As I learned from my good friend Blaine Bettinger, in every situation where unknown relationships are revealed, there are four categories of people involved: the Keeper, the Discoverer, the Subject, and the Affected. Let's look at each of these in turn.

> **The Keeper:** The person who knows the answers about how everyone is related
>
> **The Subject:** The person the secret is about
>
> **The Discoverer:** The person who first learns about the relationships
>
> **The Affected:** Anyone who has anything to do with this situation

Before I start spouting off my opinions about how things should go down, let me remind you that these are my opinions, and come from my experiences working with families in these situations and by listening to others. Ultimately, all of this DNA stuff is about connecting with people, not disconnecting. So however you orchestrate things, as long as you are working to build relationships, you are likely headed in the right direction.

OK, now that you have read my disclaimer, let me explain how I see things.

In the case of unexpected relationships, we have to balance an individual's absolute right to know their parentage or heritage with the Keeper's right to remain anonymous.

In general, we want to give the Keeper first crack at deciding how things move forward. The Keeper should have a chance to talk to the Subject themselves and explain, rather than the Subject finding out themselves or hearing it from you, the Discoverer. If you are both the Subject *and* the Discoverer, you should try to talk to the Keeper directly first, before involving other family members.

For example, I once had a client who found out the man who raised her wasn't her biological father. Her parents were very close, so my client found time to talk to her mother (the Keeper) privately, so they could discuss together how to move forward.

We could go on and on with scenario after scenario of different ways to handle different situations, but I think the best thing to do is simply follow the Golden Rule, and just do unto others as you would have them do unto you.

If your emotions are too consuming to think through a *Golden Rule* (or any) strategy, or if you're still confirming the accuracy or details of the situation, you might consider taking a little time before revealing what you've learned to anyone else affected by it. You might also consider seeking confidential support from a friend, a professional counselor, and/or within a confidential (well, as confidential as an online space can be) genetic genealogy social media space such as Facebook's DNA Surprises Support Group or DNA NPE Friends. (Find additional resources at www.watersheddna.com/resources.)

drawing on your match's tree

Marking up a printed or digital version of your match's family tree accomplishes two purposes: it helps you stay organized (by forcing you to save the tree somewhere), and it helps you stay focused on the right information in the tree. In general, your goal is to help you zero in on the generation of connection in this match's tree, and to pull out the information you need from that specific generation.

You can print out the tree and write on it with pencil (don't use a pen in case you change your mind!). Or you can take a screenshot and mark it up using tools on your computer. Or, if you are familiar with One Note or Evernote, you can use the snipping tool provided to save the pedigree to that program. It doesn't really matter how you do it; just pick a system and stick with it! Ideally, this tree will be incorporated into your research log (see page 199) as well.

Here's what you need to do:

1. Draw a box around the generation of connection you identified (and wrote down!). So, if I had determined that my generation of connection with this match was in their 16 2X great grandparents, I would draw a box around that generation. If your Best Mystery Match is in match blocks 1-9, this is good enough. If your Best Mystery Match is in match blocks 7-9, you need to expand your box to include the generation before and the generation after as there is just so much variability in cM numbers. You don't want to miss anything. I would maybe draw the most likely generation of connection in one color, and the generations before and after in a different color (but I like color!).

2. If the location of each ancestor during their childbearing years

(as best you can tell) is not visible on this family tree, write it in.

3. To the side of the pedigree, make a list of all the surnames in this generation.

At this point you may be seeing surnames or locations you recognize, which is fantastic. But BE CAREFUL. Don't jump to conclusions. Stick to the Plan and don't get ahead of yourself. Speaking of your Plan, head back over there now.

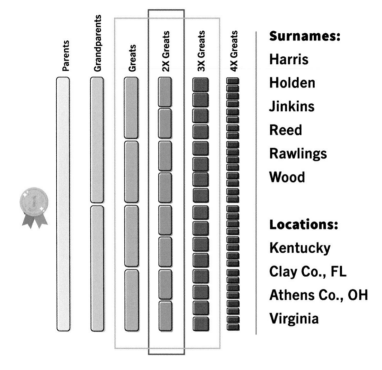

Surnames:

Harris

Holden

Jinkins

Reed

Rawlings

Wood

Locations:

Kentucky

Clay Co., FL

Athens Co., OH

Virginia

endogamy

As DNA analysis becomes more useful and mainstream in genealogy research, one group deserves special consideration. These are individuals from endogamous communities.

Endogamy is the practice by a community of marrying within its defined culture or location. Jewish and Acadian are good examples of historically endogamous communities. Endogamy is more than just a cousin marriage in your family tree. Cousin marriages can often be fairly straightforward, especially if you already know about the relationship. (See *Pedigree Collapse*, page 190 for how to adjust your shared DNA calculations for a specific instance of this phenomenon.)

But true endogamy is when you have cousin marriages repeated over and over and over again in your family history. If you have multiple recent cousin marriages (like in the last 3-4 generations) you will share too much DNA to fit into any one relationship. As mentioned in the article above, we can work around this problem when we know about it, but it is trickier when we don't know about it.

130

But as it turns out, if you are from an endogamous community and you don't have recent cousin marriages, you will still see mostly the same ranges of shared DNA as those without endogamy. But there are some clues to help you more effectively use your DNA when you are from an endogamous community.

How to Spot Endogamous Relationships

One way to help you tell the difference between someone who is closely related and someone who shares DNA because of endogamy is to pay attention not just to the total amount of DNA shared, or your relationship prediction, but to look at *the size of the pieces of shared DNA*. All of our testing companies provide this information except AncestryDNA. Please see page 204 for more information, but to summarize that page (in case you don't want to go read it), **you want that largest segment of shared DNA to be larger than 20 cM** (centimorgans). If the biggest piece is smaller than that, it is unlikely you are related recently. You can chalk up all that shared DNA to the tight-knit nature of your ancestral community, and not waste your time looking for a common ancestor.

Here's a good example. I got a new match for my grandmother at MyHeritage. This match was born in Italy, and lists in her family tree the same small town where my grandmother's mother grew up. Talk about exciting, right?! To add to my excitement was the fact that they were sharing a whopping 128 cM (my grandma's highest match, next to her niece). My grandmother was born in 1913, so this match was at least one generation younger than her, so I started working with the hypothesis that they were second cousins once removed. But after I did all the work in my Plan (yes, I follow my Plan too!) I didn't see a common ancestor. Well, long story short (or maybe it is already too long?), this match is *not* my grandmother's second cousin once removed, but instead has two (at least) more distant relationships. Now, the longest piece of DNA was 33 cM, a good big piece. But when I looked at the other pieces, and eliminated all that were under 10 cM, I was left with a total of 60 cM. That's HALF the total amount of DNA that was reported that I could consider *real*. So 60 cM came from real shared ancestors, and the other 60 likely just because we are both from northern Italy.

For the most part, filtering tools at both AncestryDNA and 23andMe are doing a very good job of eliminating the small DNA segments so that those in endogamous communities will hardly even notice an elevated amount of DNA. But if you have tested elsewhere, especially at FTDNA where we know they ARE including those small, insignificant segments, we have to be more careful.

Using Multiple Family Members to Help Sort Out Endogamy

Let's say that both of your parents are from a small town in Saskatchewan, and both of their families lived there for generations. You have a DNA match named Marie who is sharing 85 cMs with you, and you are thinking she is a 3rd cousin based on her small tree.

Here's the tip: Checking how much DNA your siblings or cousins are sharing with Marie can **sometimes** be helpful. If you see a wide variation in the amount of shared DNA between you and Marie, versus Marie and your siblings, this **may be** an indication that there is endogamy. I put the important part in bold—did you catch that? This is not a sure way to tell, just something you can check. Siblings often share varying amounts with their cousins, so this is really more of a Hail Mary, but it is something you can look at.

An even better test is to look at a first cousin. Let's say Pierre is your mom's sister's child - your first cousin. But Pierre's dad is from Québec, and therefore not mixed up in this small town Saskatchewan population. Theoretically, you and Pierre should have the same relationship to Marie (assuming Marie is related on your mom's side); she should be third cousins to both of you. But if Pierre is only sharing 22 cM with Marie, that tells you that it is very possible that some of the 85 cMs you share with Marie is coming from your dad's side as well as your mom's side.

The more relatives you have to compare, the more accurate your analysis can be.

The very, very, very most important thing to know if you are dealing with an endogamous community is that the Shared Matches tool (209) won't be able to create nice, distinct groups of matches. That's because your matches will likely be related to each other in multiple ways.

expanding your genetic network

You started your genetic network by choosing a Best Match and then running the Shared Matches tool (see page 209) to gather more matches. Sometimes the initial group of people you gathered doesn't pull in all the people that actually belong to this network. In fact, it NEVER will because of the random way DNA is inherited. While you and your sibling will have all of the same close matches, even you and your sibling will differ in your lists of third and fourth cousins. You will share DNA with some people that they will not, and vice versa. This fact is even more pronounced when you are using a more distant relative as your Best Match, as each of you will share DNA with different descendants of your common ancestor.

In this example, you can see that there are lots and lots of cousins that will be descendants of your 3X great grandparents Lionel and Lilly. But on average, you will only

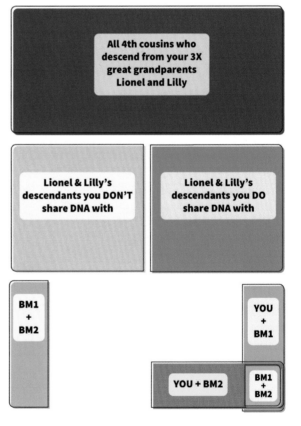

share DNA with half of them. When you use the Shared Matches tool on a third cousin Best Match (BM1) you will pick up many of those matches, but not all. If you were to expand your network by using Shared Matches with another Best Match (BM2) you will find some new matches, and some overlapping matches.

Note that if you run the Shared Matches tool between BM1 and BM2 you would be able to find additional matches that are descendants of Lionel and Lilly, but who aren't sharing any DNA with you. Unfortunately, you can only run that match-to-match shared match comparison at 23andMe. Siblings are also really good at collecting those cousins that you don't personally share DNA with. See page 138 for more on that topic.

You can keep adding related people to this network by choosing another match from the shared matches list and running the Shared Matches tool again.

But you don't have to. You can absolutely move onto the next step in your Plan without running Shared Matches on any other matches. Some indications that you may be able to just run Shared Matches once, on your Best Match:

1. Your Best Match is a first cousin or closer OR

2. You are looking for a 2X great grandparent or closer. Your Best Match is a second cousin or closer, and the Shared Matches tool found other second cousins. Having these other second cousins makes it likely that you will be able to figure out your common ancestor without the input of additional matches.

If you decide to gather more matches, you need to be oh-so-careful when you use any match to gather more matches for your network.

If possible, use only Best Matches to create your network. Meaning, **only use matches whose MRCA is the ancestor you are researching** (not possible if you are looking for a parent). Use the resources on page 105 to find them. But not all Best Matches are created equally. Now that automated tools like ThruLines can help identify Best Matches, you are going to see connections to fairly distant cousins that you may not want to use to create your genetic network.

If you have come across Tree Matches (people who share genealogy with your Best Mystery Match) in your Plan, these are also good candidates to help you expand your genetic network.

In general, before you use Shared Matches on a match to bring more cousins into your genetic network, that match has to meet the following criteria:

1. Has a documented connection to the ancestor of interest;

2. Is sharing an unsuspicious amount of DNA with you (see below);

3. As far as you can tell, is not sharing any other ancestors with you in addition to our target ancestor or ancestral couple.

What does *unsuspicious amount of DNA* mean? Well, it means that you have checked the genetic vs the genealogical relationship of this match (see page 111) and determined that it is consistent.

However, sometimes you will need to expand your network using a match for whom you are unsure of your relationship. This can increase the number of matches you believe to be related to your question, but may also gather a few matches that actually have nothing to do with your question. If your Plan has suggested this rocky path, then read on, my friend, to the next chapter. If not, forget I said any of this, and head back to your Plan.

expanding your genetic network part II

for the brave (or desperate)

When you have exhausted all of your known connections to the ancestor you are researching, and your genetic network is still pitifully small, or barren of family trees, you may need to expand your gathering techniques to try to find more matches to work with. However, be forewarned that as soon as you start using unverified matches to gather more matches, you are on shaky ground.

Here's the situation I am guessing you are in: You have gathered a group of matches into a genetic network using the methods suggested. You have looked and looked, but you can't seem to find a common connection between these cousins. So, your Plan has suggested you gather more people.

At this point, you have likely gathered all of the close cousins you can, meaning all of the second and third cousins that pertain to this line have already been found. Which means you will be mining 4th cousins for clues. If you are looking for a 2X or 3X great grandparent, this is an appropriate strategy. But if you are looking for your great grandparents, just keep in mind that you will have to do SO MUCH genealogy to get from where this bottom-of-the-barrel-match-scraping is going to start you.

Just be ready for that.

OK, so if you want to go adding people with no documented connection to the line you are searching to your genetic network, the least you can do is be responsible about it. Here's what I mean:

1. Start by labeling as many known matches from your other lines as possible as outlined in the Leftovers strategy (page 222). That way, when you use Shared Matches on one of these unverified matches, you can see if they are sharing DNA with any of your lines because they will match people who are labeled as belonging to other lines. That is not a good thing. So you probably shouldn't use that match to find new matches.

2. Pay attention to segment size and/or number. See page 204. Don't go using matches with small segments. It will likely lead you astray.

3. Minimize the chance that you are related to this match in more than one way. So if possible, find a match who only seems to have one line in the area you are researching.

4. When you have found one of these Best Matches, go ahead and use the Shared Matches tool on them, and label them. If possible, label them with the name of this match, and the name of your original network. This will help you keep these matches at least slightly separate from your "pure" network members whom you found using verified Best Known Matches.

family groups

Because each of us has our own personal mix of autosomal DNA, we are all valuable in the search for a common ancestor. So testing siblings and cousins can often improve your chances of finding that Best Mystery Match that can lead you to your ancestor.

Let me add a caveat to that: If you are looking for a grandparent, and you have already found your Best Mystery Match among your 2nd or 3rd cousins, testing more first cousins or siblings might not be necessary. That is because the matches you really need to solve this particular mystery would be first and second cousins (which you have already found), and you will likely share all of the same first and second cousins with your siblings or first cousins. Does that make sense? Let me say it another way: **You will share DNA with all of your first and second cousins, and 90% of your 3rd cousins. So testing siblings or other first cousins won't help you find new matches in those categories.**

But if you are looking for great, 2X, or 3X great grandparents, you absolutely want all of your siblings and cousins to test to help you find all of your Best Mystery Matches who are going to be in that fourth cousin category. You need everyone's help because you will only share DNA with half of your 4th cousins. Which means that all-important match with the big bushy tree who stands at the ready to answer all of your questions may not even show up on your match list. It will take the DNA of your brother or sister or cousin to find them.

But that much data can get out of hand really fast. Like *really* fast.

There are a few important things you want to look at when you test multiple family members:

Total amount of DNA shared
Because DNA inheritance is random, you are going to share different

amounts of DNA with your matches than your relatives, even your siblings. This information can be very insightful as it can help correct for some of the effects of random inheritance and keep you on the right path. For example, let's say you and your sister Pat both take a DNA test and match with John. You are sharing 125 cM with John and you are thinking you might be pretty closely related. However, when you look at the shared cMs between Pat and John, you see that they are only sharing 62 cM—HALF as much! Now, there is no telling who is "right," but it does help you adjust your thinking a bit, and allow for a more distant relationship with John than you may have first thought.

Endogamy

Sometimes comparing the DNA of multiple family members can help you sort out endogamy. For more details on how testing multiple family members can help in that situation, see page 130.

Using Close Family as A Group

In general, if you have both parents tested, your DNA (for genealogy purposes) is irrelevant. So always use the DNA of the parent, and don't be tempted to use the DNA of the child as evidence of a connection. For example, if Mark and his daughter Laura test and both match William (who you think is Mark's 3rd cousin), the fact that both Laura and Mark match William is completely irrelevant, and does not add more weight to your argument because you see two people matching William. You need to think of all close relatives (so that's you, your children, parents, siblings, even out to your first cousins) as one group. So no matter how many of you match William, that is still just ONE piece of evidence that William fits as your third cousin.

Yes, as mentioned above, it does help to look at the total amounts of shared DNA between all of your different family members to help us decide if he really is a third cousin. **But at the end of the day, the shared DNA of all of these close family members represent the DNA of one person or couple: the common ancestor (or MRCA) of your group.** Did you catch that? The DNA shared between you, your siblings, and paternal first cousin, all represents the DNA you all inherited from your paternal grandparents. Because in the end, this is really what we are trying to solve: what is the relationship between my ancestor and my match's ancestor.

To maintain your sanity, the best strategy when working with multiple family members is just to start with one, and work through your Plan using that one match. If you get stuck, or feel like a particular match needs further evaluation, turn to your family members for a second opinion.

140

finding living people

A couple of different scenarios will send you in search of information about living people:

1. Wanting to learn more about (or find other contact information for) an unresponsive DNA match.

2. Wanting to locate living individuals you have tracked down through descendancy research, in the hopes they will take a DNA test and/or provide you with genealogical information.

You can find a surprising amount of information on the internet about living people. In fact, before you use these suggestions to go find an unknown relative, **first try all of these tools by putting in your own name, or the name of a relative**. This will help you familiarize yourself with the information provided, and how accurate it is. Then move on to trying to find your cousin.

Learning more about your DNA match

Before you get started trolling the internet for details about your DNA match, you should gather as much information about your cousin as you can from the testing site. At first it may not seem like they have given you anything, but you might be surprised at the little clues they have already provided.

Specifically you are looking for name, age, location, photo and yes, even gender. First, look at your match's profile name. If it looks like a real name, it's worth pursuing the possibility. The profile name may also be a nickname or initials (which may eventually prove useful). Watch also for the name of someone who may be managing this person's DNA test for them. That person is often (not always) a relative. For example, if your match is B.H. but Juan Hernandez is the administrator, it's a fair bet B.H. shares the same surname as Juan. If your match has included a personal photo as part of their profile, you may be able to take clues from it, too, such as gender, approximate age (but watch out! Many people post pictures of themselves in their—ahem—younger years) or ethnic background.

Here's how to find all those personal details (when available) at each of our companies.

Ancestry: You need to click on a match in your match list, and then click on their name again to access their profile page. There, under their name, you will sometimes see age and *current(!)* location, but you will also see when they last logged in. You will also be able to see all public trees in their account, which may also provide clues.

MyHeritage: The age and country of location is listed right on the main match page under your match's name. Clicking on your match's name will pull up a menu; click on *View Profile*. This will bring up gender, as well as any other public information MyHeritage may have (most of which is not helpful).

23andMe: Click on your match's name to access gender, birth year, and location when available. You should also review the Family Tree feature (see page 105) to see if 23andMe has an idea of how you are connected.

Family Tree DNA: They do allow you to upload a family tree and enter surnames of interest, which can be clues to help you find out about someone. But they don't offer any further identifying information other than an email address, which can be valuable. See below.

Living DNA: Currently you can see the country of location from your Family Networks match page.

If your match has only initials, no picture, and no tree, you have two options if you want to know how they are related to you: Be patient, or ask someone else. Using the Shared Matches tool you can see others who share DNA with this match (page 209 for the Shared Matches tool). You can reach out to those matches to ask them what they know about this match of interest.

When You Know a Name

Whether you have learned the name of a relative from a DNA match profile or by doing descendancy research, there are all kinds of ways to try to figure out who they are (and how to reach them, if that is your goal). Even discovering that they have passed away can be helpful, when you find an obituary online.

Google search results: Many people have an online presence that reveals clues about their personal identities and how to contact them. Searching for their names may bring up results on LinkedIn, Facebook, employer or personal websites, news articles, and many other places. Compare what you've learned about your relative with what's apparent about the people (gender, location, age, photo) in your search results. Could they reasonably be the same person? When you Google, put the name of the person you want to find in quotes, like "Mickey Mouse." That tells Google to look for those words together.

Google Image search: If you have a name AND a profile picture, Google the name and then limit your search results to images by clicking on *Images* at the to of the search. That lets you directly compare the faces you see in search results with the DNA match's profile picture. Use any clues you have as search terms to narrow your results, such as the word "Kentucky" if that's where the person may live. This approach helped editor Sunny Morton identify a DNA match: she found and matched her profile photo on LinkedIn.

It's less likely to be effective, but you may also have luck using Google Images to search for your match's profile picture on other websites. If the testing company website allows you to right-click on your match's profile picture and save the image (like Family Tree DNA does), do that and save it to your computer. If this isn't allowed (like at AncestryDNA or MyHeritage), use your favorite screenshot tool to create and save a screenshot of your match's profile picture. Then go to https://images.google.com/. Hover over the camera icon and you'll see the option to Search by Image: choose that option. Click to upload the image. Google will search for other images just like that one. If you're lucky, it will land you on that person's LinkedIn Profile, social media page, or another place where that picture is used online.

Newspapers and obituaries: Sometimes Googling the name of the person you want to find will bring up newspaper articles referencing them (such as those found at Newspapers.com) or may bring up online obituaries and memorials, if that person has passed away. If you're specifically wondering whether a certain person is alive, it's worth Googling their name, last known place of residence and the word "obituary."

Many local public libraries also have excellent obituary files. If you know where someone may have died, you might reach out to a library's local history/genealogy section (or a reference librarian if there's no specialist).

While it can be so disappointing if you discover that a DNA match or a descendant you hoped to meet has passed away, their obituaries may prove valuable to reconstructing their family trees. Obituaries often mention the names of the deceased's parents (including mother's maiden name), children (including their married surnames) and even grandchildren. You might learn something about that person's ethnic or religious background, schooling, professional life, or other clues that may lead you to additional discoveries about them. For example, knowing the name of a person's school might help you track down an alumnus biography or yearbook photo. Repeating your Google search of that person's name with keywords about their profession may lead to career history clues that follow that person back to an unknown hometown.

People-finding websites: Websites like Been Verified (www.beenverified. com), Spokeo.com (www.spokeo.com), Pipl.com (pipl.com) and WhitePages.com (www.whitepages.com) are like online versions of a phone book, where you can look for people's contact information.

Using Been Verified as an example, once you put in the name of the person you're seeking, you will be presented with potentially a long list of possible matches. Entering as much information as you know (like place of residence) can help narrow your search. Your best resource on these sites is the list of known associates. Looking at your own report will help you better understand the people who appear on this list. For me, I see several of my husband's family on the list, even his grandfather (but neither of my sets of grandparents). When I search for my dad, I get my mom, myself, and my sister.

Before you get too excited about this: in the search results, I also see some lady in Jacksonville, FL whose name is my mom's first name, my sister's name as her middle name, and my dad's last name. But I think the naming, and the fact that my parents, my sister, and I have all lived in Florida is making this lady and several of her family members come up. So beware! These algorithms aren't always right!

The U.S. Public Records Index: Another resource for finding living (or recently-living) individuals is The U.S. Public Records Index, available on genealogy websites Ancestry.com (1950-1993, searchable in 2 separate databases), FamilySearch.org (1970-2009) and MyHeritage (1970-2010).

A description at the FamilySearch wiki reads, "This collection is an index of names, birth dates, addresses, phone numbers, and possible relatives of people who resided in the United States between 1970 and 2009. Not everyone who lived in the United States during this time will appear in the index. These records were generated from telephone directories, property tax assessments, credit applications, and other records available to the public. Birth information may be included for those residents born primarily between 1900 and 1990. These records have been gathered from multiple sources. The original sources are not available."

Other recent records at genealogy websites may also be good resources for finding a living person, such as recent phone directory listings and yearbook records.

Using Email addresses: If your testing company provides you with your match's email address, copy and paste it into your web browser. See if that email address comes up anywhere, like on a Contact webpage, professional profile or online message board.

Public online family trees: You are not likely to find living people (ie, your DNA matches or those you want to invite to test) on public online family trees. That's because most online tree systems automatically restrict tree data about people in trees who still appear to be living (no death date). That said, if a person has passed away, it's possible an online tree contains that information. AND the person who created that online tree may be a descendant—or may be able to put you in touch with a descendant. See the Genealogy Resource section, particularly the part about building a quick and simple tree (page 163), for more on searching online trees.

finding the generation of connection

You actually have two generations of connection:

1. The place on your match's tree that holds your common ancestor.
2. The place on your tree that your match's ancestor will (hopefully) fill.

So, for example, second cousins share great grandparents. Therefore the great grandparent generation is the generation of connection for both you and your second cousin match. That means one of the four great grandparent couples in your match's chart is one of the four great grandparent couples in your chart.

However, things get a little tricky when we start dealing with matches who are on a different generation than we are. In general, for matches who are younger than us, we have to look further back in their pedigree chart to find our common ancestor. The opposite is true for matches who are older than us. If you haven't already, see page 195 to find out if your match is removed from you, then come back here.

But keeping all of this straight can make your head spin. So if you want to know your generation of connection in your match's tree, find your match's suspected relationship on the chart on the next page, including if you think they are on your same generation, or older or younger. Then look to the right under the column *Your Match's Ancestor*. The ancestors listed are the ancestors in your match's chart that most likely connect to you.

Then to find the generation of connection in YOUR tree, look to the far right, under the column *Your Ancestor*. That is the ancestral couple on your YOUR tree that should be filled by the ancestor you just identified in your match's tree.

For example, if your match is your 2C1R, and younger than you, the chart tells you that one of your four sets of great grandparents should be the same as one of your match's eight sets of 2X great grandparents.

If you aren't up for just going on blind faith, and just believing me that this works, you can certainly do this on your own. I have it all laid out for you on page 151, with some helpful images about removed cousins on page 195.

Most Likely DNA-Based Relationship	Your match's generation relative to you					Common Ancestor	
	younger X2	younger	same gen.	older	older X2	Your Match's Ancestor	Your Ancestor
Full Sibling			●			both parents	both parents
Half Sibling			●			one parent	one parent
Aunt/Uncle				●		both parents	one of 2 sets of grandparents
Niece/Nephew		●				one of 2 sets of grandparents	both parents
1C			●			one of 2 sets of grandparents	one of 2 sets of grandparents
Half Aunt/Uncle				●		one parent	one of 2 sets of grandparents
Half Niece/Nephew		●				one of 4 grandparents	one parent
Great Aunt/Uncle					●	both parents	one of 2 sets of grandparents
Great Niece/Nephew	●					one of 2 sets of grandparents	both parents
Half 1C			●			one grandparent	one grandparent

Most Likely DNA-Based Relationship	Your match's generation relative to you					Common Ancestor	
	younger X2	younger	same gen.	older	older X2	Your Match's Ancestor	Your Ancestor
1C1R				●		one of 2 sets of grandparents	one of 4 sets of great grands
1C1R		●				one of 4 sets of great grands	one of 2 sets of grandparents
Half Great A/U					●	**one parent**	one of 16 great grands
Half Great N/N	●					one of 16 great grands	**one parent**
2C			●			one of 4 sets of great grands	one of 4 sets of great grands
Half 1C1R		●				one great grandparent	one grandparent
Half 1C1R				●		one grandparent	one great grandparent
1C2R	●					one of 8 sets of 2X great grands	one of 2 sets of grandparents
1C2R					●	one of 2 sets of grandparents	one of 8 sets of 2X great grands
Half 2C			●			one of 16 great grands	one of 16 great grands
2C1R		●				one of 8 sets of 2X great grands	one of 4 sets of great grands
2C1R				●		one of 4 sets of great grands	one of 8 sets of 2X great grands
2C1R			●			one of 8 sets of great grands	one of 8 sets of great grands
Half 1C2R	●					one of 32 2X great grands	one of 4 grandparents
Half 1C2R					●	one of 4 grandparents	one of 32 2X great grands
3C			●			one of 8 sets of 2X great grands	one of 8 sets of 2X great grands

Most Likely DNA-Based Relationship	Your match's generation relative to you					Common Ancestor	
	younger X2	younger	same gen.	older	older X2	Your Match's Ancestor	Your Ancestor
Half 3C			●			one of 32 2X great grands	one of 32 2X great grands
Half 2C1R				●		one of 16 great grands	one of 32 2X great grands
Half 2C1R		●				one of 32 2X great grands	one of 16 great grands
3C1R				●		one of 8 sets of 2X great grands	one of 16 sets of 3X great grands
3C1R		●				one of 16 sets of 3X great grands	one of 8 sets of 2X great grands
2C2R					●	one of 8 sets of 2X great grands	one of 32 sets of 4X great grands
2C2R	●					one of 32 sets of 4X great grands	one of 8 sets of 2X great grands
Half 2C2R					●	one of 32 2X great grands	one of 64 4X great grands
Half 2C2R	●					one of 64 4X great grands	one of 32 2X great grands
4C			●			one of 16 sets of 3X great grands	one of 16 sets of 3X great grands
5C			●			one of 32 sets of 4X great grands	one of 32 sets of 4X great grands
4C1R				●		one of 16 sets of 3X great grands	one of 32 sets of 4X great grands
4C1R		●				one of 32 sets of 4X great grands	one of 16 sets of 3X great grands
4C2R					●	one of 16 sets of 3X great grands	one of 64 5X great grands
4C2R	●					one of 64 sets of 5X great grands	one of 16 sets of 3X great grands

find the generation of connection
(the hard way)

I created the Match Block chart (see section starting on page 180) and the Generation of Connection chart ((see section starting on page 147) to make it easy for you to estimate how far back in your tree and your match's tree you need to go before you should run into your common ancestor.

So if you are still reading this, you must want to try figuring out your relationship all on your own. OK... but I am warning you, this is not for the faint of heart.

To figure out your generation of connection based on your age and your total amount of shared DNA, follow these 10 steps. Remember, you are trying to figure out which line in your match's pedigree chart holds your common ancestor. For this exercise you will need to know or be able to approximate your match's age. Remember that MyHeritage gives you this information, but at the other companies you will need to approximate (see step 2).

1. For this first exercise, print out your match's pedigree chart, or make a quick sketch of it on a piece of paper (you will want something you can write on). I am going to talk about this tree as if it is drawn like you see it here, with your match on the left, and the ancestors fanning out to the right.

2. Look at your match's pedigree chart. Based on the information

given, place yourself on the correct generation in your match's pedigree chart. Since most people don't go around posting their own birth year online, you might start by looking at the birth year of their parents. Most often, you will find one of three possibilities (though there are more):

    a.   Their parents were born in a similar era to your own parents, so you place yourself even with your match, or on the same generation as they are.

    b.   Their parents are closer to your age, so you place yourself on their parents' generation.

    c.   Their parents are your grandparents' age, and you belong one generation earlier on your match's chart. Label the relationships on your match's pedigree.

3.   Make a big star or circle or smiley face in that generation. If you seem to be falling somewhere in the middle, no worries, just make your best guess, and put yourself somewhere. Remember, this exercise is just to give you a place to start looking for your common ancestor.

    a.   Draw long vertical bar lines to separate the generations on your match's chart.

    b.   Look at you and your match on the chart. Which of you is furthest to the right on the chart. Or, to put it another way which of you is older? Put your finger on the person who is older.

    c.   Moving to the right, in the next generation after your finger, make an "X" below the chart in that generation.

    d.   In the generation after the "X" write 1st Cousin.

    e.   In the next generation, write 2nd Cousin. And so on, until you reach 4th Cousin — even if it takes you off the chart.

    f.   Put your finger back on you or your match, whichever is furthest to the right. Now look left. If there is anyone to the left of your finger, label that person with "1R."

g. If there are still people to the left of the "1R" label them "2R."

4. Take the total amount of shared DNA you share with your match to the Shared cM Project interactive tool (ScP Tool, see page 209). If you have tested at AncestryDNA, you can use their built-in calculator that I showed you how to use in the centimorgan section on page 103. This tool will produce a probability table of possible relationships for you and your match.

5. Looking at the top few tiers in the table from the ScP or from Ancestry (so those sections where the percentage likelihood is highest), cross out any relationships that are unlikely based on your age and the age of your match, as you determined in step 3. Essentially, if in step 3 you did not add any 1R or 2R labels, find those relationships in the table and cross them out. For example, if you were both born in the 50s it is unlikely that you could be their grandparent or two times removed.

Notes on step 5: If you are working in the ScP, sometimes it helps to do the above step in the chart below the table. (Go out and look at the ScP chart before you read this or it won't make any sense at all). When you enter the amount of shared DNA into the ScP tool, the chart below the table will highlight all of the relationships that are genetically possible. This is the same information that is in the table, just displayed in a different way.

Find the *Self* spot on the chart, near the middle. That is you. Every relationship on the same line as Self, going right or left, is a relationship your match could have to you if you and your match are on the same generation.

If you move down one row in the chart, and look right and left, you will see all of those relationships have a *1R* designation. That means that all of these relationships are once removed. Then the next line down says *2R* for twice removed. If you have determined that you and your match can't be twice removed, you can cross off all those relationships.

I also like how the entire left side of the chart reminds us of all the half relationships we could share with someone. **Have you considered a half relationship to your match?** A half first cousin would be someone related to only one of your grandparents. Check out page 174 if you want to learn more about half relationships.

6. In the probability table, find the relationship with the highest probability that has not been crossed out. We are going to take that relationship back to your match's chart where we have been taking notes. For example, if the relationship with the highest probability that you didn't cross out was 2C1R, then go to your match's pedigree chart and find where you have the 2nd cousin label (you should also have a 1R as the last label on the left). Put a big box around the generation you have labeled 2nd cousin. This is the first generation where you are going to start looking for your common ancestor. Or in other words, one of the couples in this generation in your match's chart could be your common ancestor.

154

Phew! Did you make it? This is a process you need to repeat over and over again before it sinks in. I recommend trying it with a Known Match, so you can see it work out with a match for whom you already know your connection.

Or, you could save yourself a lot of time and just use my table (see section starting on page 147)....

genealogy: building your own family tree

Let's start by stating the obvious: Your genetic genealogy journey has two components: genetics (DNA testing) and genealogy (your family tree). For the best experience, you need both. They work hand-in-hand to explain what the other may not be telling you.

If you have two completely unknown biological parents, your biological family tree will only take about ten seconds to build. After all, it is just you and, well, *you*.

Everyone else needs to read the following section on building your own family tree. Even if you've been doing this since before the dawn of time and you already have a family tree, at least read the numbered list in the section about two paragraphs down outlining the attributes of a DNA-testing-friendly tree.

What is a Family Tree?

A family tree file is basically an electronic diagram showing the identities of relatives and how they are related to each other. You'll use it time and again to figure out how you may be related to your DNA matches. And, importantly, having a tree activates important tools at some of your DNA testing companies that can expedite your research. Plus, it's just good genetic genealogy etiquette to have a tree linked to your DNA.

Before walking you through how to create a tree, though, you need to know the following. Don't skip over reading this list!

The best family tree for DNA matching purposes:

1. **Includes yourself.** You will be asked to link a person in the tree to the person who took the DNA test (you). That means that you need to have yourself in the family tree you are going to link.

2. **Focuses on biological branches.** Genetic relatives are the ones who are relevant to DNA testing, so just put biological relatives on this tree. This applies to your parents and your extended family.

3. **Includes both your dad's side and your mom's side.** Autosomal testing (the most common kind of DNA testing, which is where just about everyone starts) looks at both sides of your family, and so should your tree.

4. **Only needs to go back about six generations.** For the purposes of DNA matching, at least for autosomal testing, you only need to go about six generations back—and maybe not even that far back.

5. **Includes the siblings.** Try to identify not just your direct ancestors, but each of their siblings and their siblings' families (spouses and children). Your DNA matches generally descend from one of those siblings. So the more you know about them, the faster you will be able to identify your DNA matches.

6. **Comes as close to the present as possible.** Trace the descendants of those siblings as close to the present generation as possible. This becomes so beneficial when your matches don't know much about their family except for their parents and maybe grandparents.

Creating a family tree file

To create a family tree file, choose a tree-building platform. If you've tested with or are a user of Ancestry, Findmypast or MyHeritage, consider using their tree-building tools. You do not need to be a subscriber to build a tree; you just need a guest login. MyHeritage limits your free tree to 250 people—that's still a lot of relatives, so feel free to get started with it.

After subscribing or creating your free account on one of these sites, login and follow the dropdown menu choices as shown:

Ancestry: *Trees > Create and Manage Trees > Create a new tree*
Findmypast: *Family Tree > Create a tree*

MyHeritage: *Family Trees > Manage Tree > Add family tree*

You can also use family history software to build your tree. Many are available; examples include RootsMagic (www.rootsmagic.com) and Legacy Family Tree (https://legacyfamilytree.com), both of which have free downloadable getting-started versions, or Family Tree Maker (www.mackiev.com/ftm/), known for its full sync-ability with Ancestry.com.

Adding details to your family tree

Build your tree by adding basic information about your relatives, such as full name at birth and the date and place of birth, marriage and death. These unique details distinguish them from others with similar names. Start with what you know about yourself, your parents and your grandparents. (The trees will not show information on living people to others, even if your tree is public.) Then add siblings, spouses and children of each. You may not know very many details for some people. Just enter what you do know, like a first name, a year of death, a place or approximate year of birth.

Gradually research gaps in your knowledge—names, dates, places, identities of spouses or children—and add them to your tree. Begin with the present generation and work backward, building on what you learn in each generation to help identify the previous one. Look through old family papers you may have that might reveal some of these details. Ask your relatives what they recall or what old papers they may have. Watch especially for copies of obituaries; birth, marriage or death certificates; family letters or bibles; baptismal or other religious records; wills, estate or insurance paperwork and the like.

As your time and budget permit, search genealogy websites for digitized versions of old records. This process, explained briefly below, assumes you are building your tree on Ancestry.com, but the steps are similar no matter what site(s) you use.

1. In your tree, click on the relative of interest, or an unknown relative of interest, the next-of-kin (child, spouse, or parent).

For the latter situation, you'll be looking for records about the known relative that help you further identify the unknown relative.

2. Review any automatically-generated hints the site has identified. There are two kinds of hints on many genealogy websites: record hints and tree hints.

    a. Record hints are from old documents that mention someone who appears similar to your relative's description (name, associated places, etc.). It's up to you to decide whether this is really *your* person mentioned in that record (see advice below). If it is, glean any additional identifying information about that person or their relatives. With descendancy research, you definitely are focused on the children, since you're moving down the generations.

    b. Tree hints come from the family trees of other users on the site. If you're stuck, don't be afraid to look at other people's trees. They aren't always wrong! Just remember they don't necessarily know anything more than you do. A lot of people simply copy information into their trees from other trees. So don't take this information blindly. How do you know what's good? Look for trees that have a lot of historical record sources attached to ancestral profiles. Those sources provide historical evidence to support their tree data. You can usually look directly at those sources yourself—and you should.

3. After you run out of record hints, run your own searches for historical records to find any the hinting system missed. When evaluating whether a historical record pertains to your relative, watch for multiple and specific pieces of information that match what you already know—like the spouse's full name, an exact birthplace, or the names of several children. The following records are especially helpful for identifying new relatives to put on your tree (their availability may vary by time and place):

4. *Censuses.* In the United States, you can access federal census data every 10 years between 1790 and 1940. These records

are the best way to quickly reconstruct entire family groups, including all the children born over a period of years. You especially want to find all of the possible census records during your ancestor's childbearing years. Search for your family in every census, as each may mention something unique, such as the identity of a child who died young and may only appear in one census; the name of a mother-in-law who lived with the family for a time; or the name of a child's spouse, if the young couple lived with them for a time after their marriage.

5. *Birth, marriage and death records.* Collectively, in the United States, these are known as *vital records* because they report vital events in a person's life. You'll have to do a little research to know which vital records may be available for people in different times and places, as they weren't always kept in the past. These records may have been created by the government or by a church. These records help you more fully identify your relatives and connect them to each other (such as a birth record that mentions a child's parents).

6. *Obituaries.* If you can find these in newspapers, they are often an excellent resource for reconstructing families. The deceased's parents, spouse(s), siblings, children, and even grandchildren may be named. This is a good place to find married surnames for adult women. Obituaries are especially important in the United States after 1940, when census records are privacy-protected. Ask your relatives if they have any old family obituaries. Search genealogy websites for them or contact public libraries local to where the family lived; some libraries keep obituary files.

7. *Tombstones.* Tombstone inscriptions often mention a person's birth and death dates. Some relatives are buried with spouses, and sometimes you can find entire family groups buried together or at least within the same cemetery. If you can, visit these locations yourself. Search free websites such as FindAGrave.com and BillionGraves.com, which document millions of grave markers around the world. FindAGrave entries sometimes link to the entries of spouses, siblings, and children and sometimes

obituaries have been transcribed here. If possible, verify the obituary contents by finding your own copy of it and verify in other records (such as the ones listed above) whether those hyperlinked relatives really are theirs.

8. Still striking out? Try looking for relatives' names in old newspapers, including within the pages of digitized newspapers at sites such as (in the United States) the free Chronicling America website (https://chroniclingamerica.loc.gov/) or subscription sites such as Newspapers.com or GenealogyBank.com.

As you find each piece of information about each person, don't forget to add it to your family tree! The more you learn about each relative, the more you may be able to learn about that person's relatives, too. Many who build family trees also attach digitized photos and stories to relatives' tree profiles. Doing so helps you (and your DNA matches who view them) better identify and feel connected to them. But they're not strictly necessary for the DNA matching experience to work. Remember, the goal of creating a family tree for DNA purposes is not a complete life sketch, but to identify as many relatives as possible, going back about 6 generations.

If you are working with a family tree on Ancestry or MyHeritage that is directly connected to your DNA profile, you won't need to update your tree file (the site does it automatically). But if you're uploading a family tree file from some other software and attaching it to your DNA test, you'll want to periodically update that tree file at your DNA testing company by replacing it with your most recent tree file from your computer.

Those new to genealogy may find this section overwhelming. The good news is that you (usually) don't need to be an expert to build a family tree that is at least somewhat helpful for DNA testing. If you do get stuck, there's an enormous community of friendly genealogy lovers out there who would likely be happy to help you. Find them by Googling "find a genealogy society near me;" asking at your local public library; or finding a free Family History Center near you (search for one at www.familysearch.org/locations/).

genealogy: descendancy research

Building a Tree from the Past to the Present

When you come forward in time on your family tree by documenting the posterity of your great-aunts and uncles (and great-greats, etc.), that's called descendancy research. You may find yourself doing descendancy research either on your own tree OR on your match's tree. You'll do this for your match's tree when you need to bring that tree forward in time to identify your connection OR when you need to find living relatives.

For your own family, look in your tree for great-aunts and uncles (and then great-grand aunts and uncles, etc.) who are just dangling there with no spouse or children. Use the steps outlined in the section on tree-building to find their children, then their children's spouses and children, etc. Once you make it to the present, you can employ the tactics in the Finding Living People section (page 141) to fill in the current generations of your tree.

To trace the descendants of someone who's not yet in your tree (like, your match's ancestor), you can start a new tree on Ancestry.com, or wherever you are doing your tree-building. Then follow all the steps already outlined in the tree building section. You may also consider skipping down to the *Quick and Simple Tree* on (page 163) for tips on how to harvest other people's tree data.

Descendancy research helps with DNA matches. Let's say you have a new DNA match named Marcia Noel. She has a very small pedigree posted with just her parents and one set of grandparents. You see that her grandmother's name is Mary Rickarts. If you haven't taken just that little bit of extra time to understand all of the descendants of your known ancestors, you may find yourself sighing with disappointment that you have yet another DNA match with a tiny pedigree for whom you don't know your relationship. However, if you did your homework, you will recognize that one of your great-grandmother's sister's daughters (did you follow that?) married a Rickarts. Ah-ha! **Known to unknown as a result of building the best possible family tree.**

genealogy: quick and simple tree

See How DNA Matches Connect To Each Other

To do genetic genealogy, you have to have a tree for your DNA match that stretches back far enough so you can see the ancestor you have in common. Unfortunately, most matches just haven't done that much genealogy. But, you may be in luck thanks to a pretty nifty principle about modern populations: we all came from a relatively small pool of ancestors. **That means that the ancestor you see in your match's tiny tree is likely also present on someone else's (hopefully much larger) tree.**

Building a quick and simple tree is all about finding an online tree that has more information about your match's ancestors than your match does. When your match has a stub of a tree, you can often expand this tree by searching online trees created by other genealogists to see what they have already discovered about your match's ancestor. Now don't forget: relying on other people's trees is not good genealogy scholarship (that means it's a big no-no). But it's a common practice in genetic genealogy when you are just trying to see a connection between a group of people who share DNA. You should think of these as theories. If your grafted-together tree seems to blossom (meaning this larger tree allowed you to see common ancestors among your matches), then you can go ahead with additional research in traditional records to make sure you are right.

> **Important:** *Why you might be wrong.* Let's say your match George heard from his second cousin's wife's brother's mother-in-law who is somehow related to your family (you don't want me to go into how you are related to her, trust me) that your 2X great grandfather is Lewis Marshall. So George puts Lewis in his tree. Dean, a newbie genealogist, copies this name into his tree. Carol

sees Lewis in the Dean's and George's tree, and then goes and finds a record that has the name Lewis Marshall on it (never mind that the dates don't quite line up) and based on George's tree, Dean's tree, and this new record, puts Lewis in her tree.

So then you come along and you see DNA matches with George, Dean, and Carol. You see the common ancestor Lewis Marshall in their trees and you think: BAM! I found my ancestor! Do you see how this whole quick and simple tree thing can be problematic? The important thing to keep in mind here is that you share DNA with George, Dean, and Carol, and it is likely that you share a common ancestor. But only by doing actual genealogy research can you be sure of the name of that ancestor. **What you get from your quick and simple trees is just a hint.**

If you want to try this out, it may help to start a new tree for this DNA match in your genealogy software or online—wherever you keep your family trees. If you are creating it online, make sure you mark the tree as private (for now, while you're building it) so other genealogists won't stumble upon this working tree. Then get to work! Search online trees for the names you see on your match's tree stump. Start with specific searches and gradually broaden them as needed to cast your net a little wider.

Several major websites host entire forests of online trees. If you have already created your match's tree online, start at the website where you created it, as their record and tree hinting tools will likely come in handy. If not, here's my suggested course to follow.

FamilySearch

Start here because it is free. And, well, free is good.

FamilySearch.org hosts one giant family tree of the world, to which more than 5 million people have contributed. You can glean information from the FamilySearch Tree in two ways:

1. Use the search feature to look for any deceased person named on your match's tree. Under the Search menu, choose Family Tree. Then enter the names and other identifying information about a deceased relative. The search system will bring up likely matches, which you can click on to review. You'll look for two things: personal details about that person AND links to that person's immediate relatives (parents, children, spouses). Tip: within an individual's profile, click View Tree to see at-a-glance anything known about that person's relatives.

2. Participate in the Family Tree yourself. Create a free Family-Search login at FamilySearch.org and follow the prompts to begin building a family tree. The difference on this site is that you're not creating an individual tree: you're building yourself INTO their global public tree. You'll just enter your parents' and grandparents' names (etc.) until you find deceased ancestors who are already in the Family Tree. Link yourselves to them. Then, as mentioned above, look to see what already exists for that person in the form of tree data (descendants or ancestors or both!). Note: what you enter about living people in the Family-Search Family Tree will be privacy-protected. Information about deceased people will be viewable by others.

Once you've found ancestors on the FamilySearch Family Tree, you can't just download a certain branch of the family and graft it into your tree (wouldn't that be nice!). You'll have to either manually enter what you find into your tree or download a tree of all your recent ancestors (and their descendants) by following the instructions at www.yourdnaguide.com/ydgblog/2019/11/13/download-your-family-tree-from-familysearch.

Two other websites offer a free, global family tree experience: Geni.com (owned by subscription site MyHeritage) and WikiTree.com. Follow the instructions on these sites to search for ancestral names.

Ancestry.com and MyHeritage.com

These two companies have very similar tree setups, and both require a paid subscription to fully access other users' online trees. As opposed to FamilySearch's single online public tree, these two genealogy giants allow their users to create individual trees, which may or may not be publicly viewable. That means that when you search for the ancestor of your match, you may see several online family trees that contain this ancestor (or at least someone who looks like him or her). Prioritize those that have more sources listed, but look closely at all trees that appear to have information you don't yet know.

You can't download someone else's tree (or part of a tree) on Ancestry or MyHeritage. So any information you find on others' trees, you'll have to manually enter into your own tree (or for a separate tree you may create for your match: see below for shortcuts).

How can you tell that the person mentioned in an online tree is the same as the person in your match's tree? Often your match hasn't given you much to go on. So you compare the things you can see. Things like places of birth and death, names of spouses and parents and children. Even if you are reasonably certain you have found the right person in an online tree, how can you be certain the other information provided is correct? Well, you can try to find trees that have documentation and cited sources. If they lack those essentials, you can try to find the documents yourself. Use the same strategies outlined previously for finding and evaluating records.

Keep in mind the purpose of this quick and simple tree: to show you how your matches are related to each other. You are looking for common names and locations between your matches that can give you a clue as to your connection with them. So don't get too caught up in dotting i's and crossing t's in other people's trees. Just find what you need to know and move on with your burning DNA questions.

Creating a quick and simple tree for your DNA match in your Ancestry account:

At Ancestry and MyHeritage, there's a faster way to create a tree for your match that you can build upon yourself. After logging in at each site, create a tree:

Ancestry.com: *Trees > Create and Manage Trees > Create a new tree*
MyHeritage.com: *Family Trees > Manage Tree > Add family tree*

In the new tree, add the name of your Best DNA Mystery Match (or any other match you might be building a tree for) as the home person. I usually start their name with "DNA" and then add their username or full name. If a generation or more is living and therefore privacy protected, just build skeleton profiles for them called "unknown mother," "unknown father," etc., and continue backward on the tree toward generations that actually have names.

When you get to the first deceased and therefore identified person on their tree, you'll have to manually copy over from MyHeritage whatever information is in your match's tree profile about that person. On Ancestry, just enter the name information. Then on the match's tree, click on the name of the deceased person you just added to bring up his or her profile page. Click on *tools* in the upper right corner, then *Save To Tree*. Choose your newly-created tree from the list of options and start typing the name of the individual to find them in your tree. Then click Save. All the information about that person will then be moved to your new tree, without having to key it in.

You may need to enter a few deceased people before the Ancestry or MyHeritage site thinks to itself, "Hey, I've seen this tree data before." When this happens, you'll see hints appear pertaining to their profiles. Hopefully, one of those hints is the online tree for your match (or another user) that contains the parents, siblings, and other children of this ancestor. So click on the tree hints (on MyHeritage these are called Smart Matches), review the information, and accept the hints to quickly add generations back to your generation of connection. Remember, this is a TERRIBLE way to do genealogy, but an excellent way to build out your DNA match's tree to quickly see a connection between members of your genetic network.

generating trees for groups of DNA matches

When you find a group of matches who have a common ancestor with each other, you need to get all of those people drawn out on a tree so you can see where you might fit in. There are lots of ways you can do this, and some methods work better in some situations than in others. I will list a few here. But the important thing is that once the chart is drawn, you are able to check the genealogical vs. the genetic relationships you have with each match. That is done automatically through the WATO tool, which is first on our list below. But it is very helpful if you know how to do it yourself, both so you can double check your work in WATO, and so you can draw your own trees outside of WATO if you want to. See page 111 for more information on checking the genetic vs. the genealogical relationship.

WATO
www.DNApainter.com/tools

This tool is called What Are The Odds and it is a powerful way to explore how you might be connected to a group of DNA matches.

This free tool lets you draw a pedigree chart for your related DNA Matches, including the amount of DNA they share with you. You can then add hypothetical locations in the tree where you might belong. The tool will tell you if your hypothesis is genetically possible and how likely it is that one of your hypothetical relationships is better than another.

Let's try it with some matches in a genetic network who all seem to descend from an unknown-to-you ancestral couple, Jamal and Jada. In the WATO image below are four DNA matches whose genealogy indicates their relationships to Jamal and Jada as shown.

We have also entered the amount of DNA they share with us. Then we added your ancestor Edmonia to two places on the tree where we think she could fit: as the full sister of Lorna, James, and Tyree (pink dotted line, leading to Hypothesis 3) and as their half-sister (yellow dotted line leading to Hypothesis 2). We also threw in a third hypothesis (Hypothesis 1) just for fun.

You can see that Hypothesis 1 is red and has a score of zero, meaning it is not genetically possible given the amount of DNA shared with the people on the chart. However, the other two hypotheses are possible.

The score of "4" on Hypothesis 3 means that it is 4 times more likely that Edmonia is the full sister of Lorna, James and Tyree, meaning she is the child of both Horace and Hattie, as opposed to the half sibling of Lorna, James and Tyree (meaning that only Horace OR Hattie would be her parent). But since both are possible, how do you know which one is the true relationship? You could test more descendants of this family and enter them into the tool (see targeted testing on page 224), or you could do genealogy research, looking for records connecting you (and Edmonia) to Horace and Hattie.

I try to use WATO whenever possible, and I want you to do the same. All of your WATO trees are saved in your free online account. You can even save an image of the tree to your digital research log, or share your tree with a relative. Stick with WATO unless:

- You and your match have multiple relationships. WATO doesn't have any way for you to take that into account.

- You want to include matches who are descendants of a married couple's parents. It is difficult to put that into WATO as you can only have one common ancestral couple on the very left, and in that situation you would need two. But you can just make two WATO charts.

Some other options, just in case, but really, stick with WATO if you can.

Lucidchart.com
www.lucidchart.com

This tool is mostly free and uses a simple drag-and-drop interface to let you build your family tree. I will often add the name of the match, and the total amount of DNA that is shared.

170

Lucid Chart also has a hot spot functionality that lets you include external links to other pages. So you could add a hot spot link to a match in your tree that will take you directly to their match page at the testing company, or to an online family tree that contains more details.

Pencil and Paper

Hey, nothing wrong with kickin' it old school! The most important thing to remember is to keep all of the generations aligned. You need to be able to see when someone is once removed or twice removed - so keep all of that stuff straight.

getting unstuck

Even though I have tried to carefully outline most foreseeable scenarios, the nature of DNA dictates that I just can't plan for everything. So gathered here are some resources you should consider tapping into before you throw in the proverbial towel. However, sometimes you just need a break! Take some time away from this problem and come back to it in a few days or a few weeks with fresh eyes.

A. Start again. This is kind of like a reboot of your computer. Go back to step one and try to go through the process again, with new eyes, to see if perhaps there is something you missed.

B. Review the ethnicity results, paying close attention to any genetic communities at Ancestry. For example, if you are looking for your grandfather, and your ethnicity report says you are 22% Italian, and you don't have any other Italian ancestors, it is very likely that your missing person was Italian. If you are looking for a great grandparent, or even a great great grandparent and you know your ancestor was from Germany, you can look for other matches who have German heritage, or who live in Germany now (made easier by tools at MyHeritage DNA, Living DNA, and 23andMe, see page 201).

C. If you can't see common surnames or locations right away, try using the location tools at various companies to help and look for matches who are from the areas you are researching.

D. If you can't find a common ancestor among your genetic network, consider that the genealogy of the matches you have been working with may be wrong. (Gasp! Can you believe it? Someone else's research is incorrect?!) But I am not talking about genealogy mistakes, I am talking about genetic, er, incongruities. Where the paper says they are related to the ancestor on the chart, but they are not. If this is the case, there isn't much you can do, except contact them and gently inquire about their family. But then again, this might be your DNA sending you a signal that this line has at least some level of endogamy. Head over to page 130 to read about that.

E. Remember that your generation of connection is not set in stone. Try to move the connecting generation back one generation. Then do genealogy research, looking for connections between your genetic network(s).

F. If you can't find a common ancestor in your genetic networks, you may take a gander at the segment size on page 204 to see if perhaps the matches you are looking at might not be Best Matches, or matches for whom you can reasonably expect to find a shared ancestor based on their segment number or size.

G. Do more of your own genealogy. Finding the spouses and children of your ancestor's siblings (we call these collateral lines) is a great way to familiarize yourself with surnames that you might see on your DNA match list, and therefore help you find out where a match fits in your tree. See page 155.

H. Bring in reinforcements in the form of your sibling or cousin (page 138). Run through the Plan again to gather more matches from the view of this additional person to see if you can find a new Best Mystery Match to help you solve your problem.

I. Did you read the section on YDNA (page 232) and mtDNA (page 184)? Would either of those tests be helpful in this situation?

J. How about targeted testing? Remember that all of your cousins will have a slightly different DNA record than you do. Perhaps their tests will find you the match you need. Head over to page 224 to read all about targeted testing.

K. Have you tested at all available companies including 23andMe, AncestryDNA, Family Tree DNA, MyHeritage DNA, and Living DNA? You can actually transfer your results for free from any company to Family Tree DNA and MyHeritage DNA (see www. yourDNAguide.com/transferring for more information). Testing at multiple companies may help you find that one DNA match that cracks your case wide open.

L. Tell this story. No matter how far you got in this journey, it is a story worth telling. You don't need to know the end in order to write the beginning. Flip over to page 226 for some ideas.

M. Ask for help. You can try your local genealogy society, online Facebook forum, or perhaps a nearby genealogy conference. In the end, the fastest way to accurate answers is to ask an expert. Your DNA Guide offers expert research packages to help get you unstuck and moving back along your Plan. See www.yourDNA-guide.com/mentoring for more details.

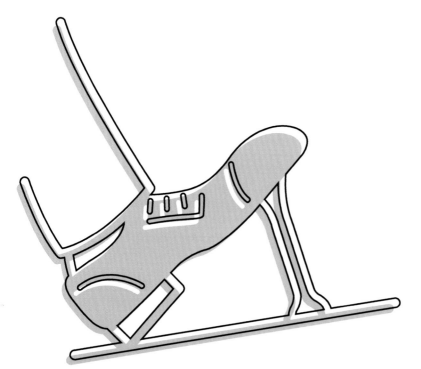

half relationships

As if you needed one more complication....

Half cousins share only one of the two ancestors in an ancestral couple. Most people understand a half sibling, where only one parent is shared. But it is more difficult to think about a half second cousin.

Let's use an example. Let's say that Naji and Kisha are half second cousins. Who is their shared ancestor? It helps to first think about the ancestral couple that would be shared if they were full second cousins. Full second cousins share great grandparents (see page 147 and the generation of connection chart for more). Let's say the common great grandparent couple for Naji and Kisha is Amar and Adah.

Now, if instead of being full second cousins sharing BOTH Amar and Adah, if Naji and Kisha are only half second cousins, they share only one of these people as their ancestor. They are both descendants of either Amar OR Adah.

174

Sometimes you know to be on the lookout for half cousins because you know that your great grandpa Richard died in the Civil War when Roslyn was just barely pregnant with your grandfather. She then married Ronald and had five more kids. So you know that all of the descendants of those kids will be your half second cousins.

Unfortunately, many times these half relationships aren't nearly as well documented as Roslyn's application for her widow's pension which lays out in detail all the facts you need to make all of the connections. Many times half relationships pop up in undocumented situations (a father might never even have known he had a son or daughter, and either parent may have concealed the existence of a child), which can make them much more difficult to identify.

Best thing to do as you are following your Plan is to keep an open mind, and let the DNA make suggestions for you to investigate. So, go jump back on the path and just remember what you have learned about half relationships.

175

labeling matches

Once you find matches you want to add to your genetic network (see page 209) you will need to label them so you can use them later.

Deciding what to name each new group is more complicated, because the possibilities might be endless. But, since I know endless possibilities are not very helpful, let's make things a bit more concrete. How you choose to label your matches really depends on why you are reading this page. I see three possible scenarios:

A. You just used the Shared Matches or ICW tool on a Best Mystery Match and you need to label the resulting list as being related to the Best Mystery Match. The easiest place to do this is in the resulting list itself: you can just go down this list and mark them all.

B. You are employing the Leftovers Strategy (see page 222) and you are trying to label everyone in your match list who is NOT related to your match in question.

C. You are just studying up and thought this chapter sounded fun (you overachiever!).

No matter your scenario, you can choose to label each group with the surnames of the ancestors you share with this Best Mystery Match (if you know them, that is), like *Haselwood + Dance*. But if you don't know your shared couple, then just label this group with the name of your Best Mystery Match like *Sharing with Marcus Fiddlebunk* (where Marcus is the name of your Best Match).

When you are trying to comprehensively label every person on your match list with the label of your known ancestors, as in the Leftovers strategy, it helps to have a plan in place before you start. Personally, I like to label DNA cousins as they relate to each of my four great grandparent couples and each of my eight 2X great grandparent couples. Or, if I am aiming to find a 2X great, I label all the 2X and 3X greats. As I mentioned, I name them with the two surnames of that couple, like *Haselwood + Dance*.

> **Some deep thinking:** If you want to think of it a bit deeper, when you label a second cousin using this system, that second cousin should end up with THREE labels: one for your shared great grandparents, and one for each of the two 2X great grandparents that you share. A third cousin would only have one label: for the one set of 2X great grandparents you share.

Sound good? Take home principle is this: Every couple gets a color.

Labeling matches is easiest at AncestryDNA, and this process is described below. But it is necessary no matter where you are finding your matches. So, for labeling at all other companies, I have two suggestions (and you will likely want to use both): first, use the notes feature at your company. When you run Shared Matches, label each one with a group name in the notes field. Secondly, you could keep lists of these groups of shared matches in a separate document, spreadsheet, or as a digital note in One Note or Evernote, if you use these tools. Whatever you do, you just need to know who these people are so you can be sure you are including them in your analysis.

That's it! Done! Well, almost done. If you haven't tested at AncestryDNA, jump down to the *Possible Problems with Labeling* section. For those of you who have tested with AncestryDNA (and for those of you reading for fun) let's find out more about the labeling system at Ancestry.

Labeling Matches in Groups at Ancestry

First of all, if you have had either of your parents tested, Ancestry will automatically label the matches that belong to that parent. But remember, if you are doing research on your mom's side, and she has tested, you are irrelevant, so stop looking at *your* match page!

Adding a match to a group at Ancestry is as simple as clicking the + *Add to group* button on the right side of the match, and choosing a group. (You'll see in the same spot an option to create each new group, as needed.)

You can create up to 24 labels at AncestryDNA. Labels for 4 great grandparent couples and 8 great grandparent couples uses 12 of these. I would love to be able to add my 16 3X great grandparent couples to that list, but alas, that is over my color limit (argh! couldn't they just add four more colors?!). So I have to pick and choose which of the 3X greats get labels. Or, if I know I am going to need to work with fourth cousin matches (if I am looking for a 3X great grandparent), then I remove the dots from the great grandparents, and use them for the 3X greats, as shown in the image.

If you follow this system perfectly, then your full siblings will have all 24 colors marked (as they are descendants of all lines), while your second cousin will have three dots, one for the great grandparent couple they descend from, and two for the two 2X great grandparent couples they descend from. As you can see, how many dots a person has can actually reveal information about your relationship to them - but we will save that discussion for a later time.

The point is: choose a system and stick with it. Keeping track of these matches is central to all of the work you are doing here, so consistency is key.

Possible Problems with Labeling

Sooner or later, you are going to run into a situation where someone you have labeled as related to a maternal side ancestor shows up in a shared matches list with a paternal side ancestor. Most of the time this is totally ok. Remember from your shared Matches lesson that people are often related to others in the network in multiple ways. The important thing as far as labeling is concerned is to ADD THE LABEL. Let them both be there. Labeling is all about just marking what you see. You will figure out what it all means later.

Having said that, there are some key times when the presence of multiple labels is your DNA trying to tell you something important about your relationship. For example, it is very possible that you do have two relationships to a DNA match, instead of just one. For example, I have a DNA match who is both my 2C and my 3C1R. This is important for us to know, so if you see multiple labels, take a quick second to scan the pedigree of this match to look for multiple relationships.

All right, everyone, head back to your Plan and keep moving! And if you are just reading for fun...I guess just keep going!

match blocks

While the amount of total DNA shared is important and you can use it to help better define your relationships, DNA is too unpredictable for us to be relying on it too heavily. So instead of thinking about a total amount of shared DNA as definitely defining a particular relationship, it is more accurate to think of an amount of shared DNA landing you in a relationship block. This block will reveal the handful of most likely relationships that you should evaluate as the genealogical connection between you and your match. Note that I did not say that this list is the be-all-end-all list of your possible relationships. Just that these are the ones we will start with. Determining which relationship is genealogically correct depends on lots of factors, but a big one is just how old you are compared to how old your match is.

Before I even show you the table I made that I know you are going to be excited about, I need to insert this disclaimer and get your cross-your-heart-and-hope-to-die promise that you will use this table responsibly. Promise?!

disclaimer

I have laid out some definite numbers because I know how much you crave defined limits. But in all honesty, we just can't talk about DNA relationships in such defined terms with such sharp edges. In reality, when we get past Match Block 2, all of the lines are blurred and there is so much overlap that it is almost scandalous for me to create this list. It goes against every scientific bone in my body to see this in black and white. But I did because I know you want to be told what to do (if only my children were more like you…). Please just remember that these ranges are not in any way set in stone, but are meant to be used as a guide to help you know where to START looking for your common ancestor. That's it! **That's the whole point of this exercise of looking at shared cMs: to give you a starting point for your research.**

OK, let's take a look at the table. You can see for each block I have indicated a minimum and maximum cM number (did I mention these could not possibly be correct in all cases and that there is so much room for other interpretations?). Then you see a list of best-fit relationships when you take into account the generational difference between you and your match that you should have determined already. If you didn't, head over to page 195 and figure that out before you move on.

Block	min cMs	max cMs	Your match's generation relative to you				
			younger X2	younger	same generation	older	older X2
1	3000	3500		Child		Parent	
2	2200	2999			Full Sibling		
3	1200	2199		Niece/ Nephew	Half Sibling	Aunt/ Uncle	
4	650	1199	Great N/N	Half N/N	1C	Half A/U	Great A/U
5	340	649	Half Great N/N	1C1R	Half 1C	1C1R	Half Great A/U
6	200	339	1C2R	Half 1C1R	2C	Half 1C1R	1C2R
7	90	199	Half 1C2R	2C1R	Half 2C	2C1R	Half 1C2R
8	60	89	2C2R H2C2R	H2C1R 3C1R	3C H3C	H2C1R 3C1R	2C2R H2C2R
9	20	59	4C2R	4C1R	4C 5C	4C1R	4C2R

I created this table with data from the AncestryDNA Matching white paper and the Shared cM Project which was created by Blaine Bettinger (my dear, dear friend) and then made available as a fancy interactive tool by the brilliant Leah Larkin and the talented Jonny Perl. See www. yourDNAguide.com/scp for more information, or you can visit page 207 to learn about using the Shared cM Project Tool yourself. You should definitely do that if you are feeling skeptical about my table, and you want to go out and run some numbers for yourself (go for it! I love data!).

> **Removed?** Now, it isn't always possible to tell if you are or are not on the same generation. If you don't know, just start with Same. But if you can see that your match is 40ish and you are 70ish, it is very possible that your match is one generation younger than you are. So start with that listed relationship as your working hypothesis about your connection, and move out from there.

Just to let you know how terrible these ranges are at actually placing matches in the right relationship ranges, I used this very table I am encouraging you to use to look up a handful of relationships I know I have to some of my DNA matches. The table placed them in the wrong match group about half (yup, you read that right - HALF) of the time. But, many of them were right on the edge of a match group. For many the table told me that their most likely relationship was a half relationship, when the real relationship was a full relationship in the match block above or below it. For example, I had a 2C1R who shared 206 cM, placing him in match block 6, with a most likely relationship of H1C1R. You can see from the table that 206 is just a tad bit too much for match block 7 where he belonged. So if you have a match who is on the edge of a match group, make sure you look at the block either above or below for other likely relationships, and don't be a slave to the table! It is a guide, not a crystal ball.

I highly recommend you read the section on page 207 about the Shared Centimorgan Project and about AncestryDNA's probability tables on page 103. Use these tools in conjunction with my Match Block table to help you know a good relationship to begin with, which will hopefully take you down the shortest path to your common ancestor.

One last thing, just because I can't resist, it is just so sciency! I am throwing in this chart created by AncestryDNA in their Matching White Paper published in 2016 that shows you how much overlap there is between shared amounts of DNA and relationships. Each color in the chart represents different relationships. They talk about it in terms of meioses, but you don't even need to know what that means. All that matters is the separation between these categories.

Starting at the top and moving down you can see that the dark blue line at between 340 and 650 cM is the last distinct line. Check out the spot on the chart I have highlighted. You can see that by the time we get to the middle of the green peak, we can see green, yellow, black, light blue, and purple. Remember, each color represents multiple relationships. So that means in this section between say 200 and 90 cMs there are at least 10 possible relationships and if we scoot down to the 40-90 cM range those relationship categories are almost indistinguishable. Take home message: DNA inheritance is

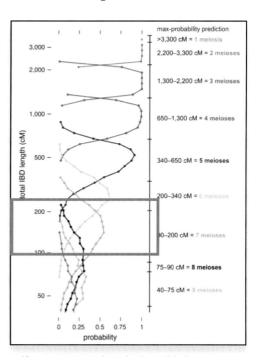

If you want to take a look at this image (and lots of others) in the AncestryDNA Matching White Paper (fascinating!) you can find it here: https://www.ancestry. com/corporate/sites/default/files/ AncestryDNA-Matching-White-Paper.pdf

unpredictable, so be flexible in your interpretations.

mtDNA basics

Mitochondrial DNA (mtDNA) is a small, circular piece of DNA that absolutely everyone has. It is 16569 DNA letters long (the letters represent the four different building blocks of DNA which are A, T, C, and G). We get this mtDNA from our mothers,

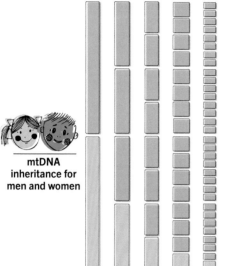

mtDNA inheritance for men and women

who got it from their mothers, who got it from their mothers, and so on. That means that the mtDNA you are carrying around in your body right this second is likely exactly the same mtDNA that your mother had, and even the same mtDNA that your 8X great grandmother had.

Unless it's not.

At every generation there is a chance of mutation. That means that one of those DNA letters has changed. This is a totally normal, albeit infrequent, occurrence, and it usually doesn't actually mean anything for you, the user of this mtDNA. But over time these mutations have left a pattern of relationships, dividing the world into hundreds of different mtDNA lineages that each have their own path and story.

In the Lab

The mtDNA can be divided into three sections: HVR1, HVR2, and the Coding Region. The HVR regions usually experience the most mutations, but there is a fair amount of activity happening in the Coding Region as well.

Each mtDNA is sequenced in the lab—meaning they find the exact arrangement of As, Ts, Cs, and Gs. However, in a full sequence test, the recommended test for genetic genealogy, each person would have 16569 letters to report! As that seems like just a little bit too much information to display nicely on a webpage, the company instead compares your values to a reference sequence, and then only reports to you the differences from that sequence, as shown above. What is reported to you is the position of the difference, and your value at that location. Your mtDNA profile then is just your collection of differences from this reference sequence.

mtDNA matching

When you share the same mtDNA profile, it means that at some point in time, you likely share a direct maternal line with that match. The problem is, your connection could be very recent, or very distant, and it is very hard to tell the difference.

For the most part, mtDNA is useful in combination with autosomal DNA testing. It can help you decide how you might be related to an autosomal DNA match. For example, if you are sharing autosomal DNA with someone, and you have been predicted to be third cousins, that means you connect at one of your 16 2X great grandparent couples. That's a lot of choices that need investigating! But if you also share the same mtDNA profile, then instead of evaluating 16 couples for a possible connection, the first place to start looking would be on your direct maternal line 2X great grandparents, and your match's direct maternal line 2X great grandparents.

haplogroups

Only testing company Family Tree DNA reports the full mtDNA sequence data—or an mtDNA profile that would contain every possible mtDNA value you can test and is great for mtDNA matching. But there is a second kind of result that helps us figure out where your ancestor may have been a really, really, really long time ago. It is called a haplogroup.

Your mtDNA haplogroup is included as part of your test at 23andMe, and part of the Ancestry Kit at Living DNA. It also comes with your purchase of any mtDNA test at Family Tree DNA.

A haplogroup is a deep ancestral group usually associated with a general geographic location. While most haplogroup origins are too far back to be helpful in determining where your maternal line ancestor is specifically from, it can help you determine the answers to specific questions about your direct maternal line connections to big pieces of land (like continents) or to specific groups of people (like Native Americans).

the short of it

All you really need to know is this: Your mtDNA haplogroup might be useful if you are wondering if your direct maternal line was from Africa or if you are Jewish or Native American. Your mtDNA profile (available only at FTDNA) might help you find someone who shares your direct maternal line, but then again, it may not. The best way to use mtDNA in the scope of this book is to look for autosomal DNA matches who are sharing the same mtDNA haplogroup (available at FTDNA, 23andMe, and Living DNA) when you are researching your direct maternal line.

multiple relationships

If you have been diligently creating your genetic networks as outlined in your plan, but are just having trouble isolating the line you are going after, it might be because you and your Best Known match or your Best Mystery Match have multiple relationships to each other.

This is a little bit different from pedigree collapse where two related people in your tree marry and have children. As we saw in that section (page 190) if that relationship is a couple generations back in your pedigree, the added amounts of DNA are usually not significant enough for you to notice, and you can pretty much go through your Plan without a hitch.

However, it is also possible to be related to a match in two ways through unrelated lines. And this can significantly impact how effective the Plan will be in your research.

Multiple Relationship Case Study

Let's take the example of Russ and Peg who have two daughters, Mary and Ruby. Mary marries Joe and they have baby Ruth (get it - Baby Ruth? Like the candy?). But then Mary dies of the measles and Joe ends up marrying Ruby, and they have Gus. So, this means that Gus and Ruth have TWO relationships to each other. They are half siblings through Joe, and also first cousins through their

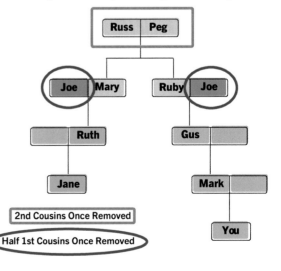

mothers. But we aren't testing Ruth and Gus, we are testing you and Jane. So what two relationships do you and Jane have? Now, I threw in a removed, just for fun (if you don't yet think removeds are fun, go read the section about Removed Cousins on page 195). But don't let it throw you. Just calculate the relationships for Jane and Mark, and then add a 1R afterwards.

Jane and Mark are second cousins through their great grandparents Russ and Peg. So that makes you and Jane second cousins once removed (2C1R). According to the Shared Centimorgan Project (ScP, see page 207) 2C1R share an average of 123 cM.

Now for your second relationship. Jane and Mark are also half first cousins because of their shared grandfather Joe. So that makes you and Jane half first cousins once removed (H1C1R). The ScP says the average amount of shared DNA for H1C1R is 226 cM.

Here's the kicker: When you are looking at the total amount of shared DNA between you and Jane on the match page at your testing company, having these two relationships can often give you a total cM amount much higher than either one of your true relationships. In this case, you and Jane are sharing 349 cM. Take a look:

	Relationship	Average shared cMs	Observed range of shared cM (from ScP)	Calculated shared cM (cMs from A+B)	Total shared cM reported by the testing company
You & Jane	A 2C1R	A 123 cM	A 0 - 316		
	B H1C1R	B 226 cM	B 57 - 530	349 cM	328 cM

So when you encounter Jane in your match list, and you are unaware of the whole Joe and Mary and Ruby thing, you will take that total amount of shared DNA into the ScP and see that it is 53% likely that you are first cousins once removed (1C1R), which she isn't. Assuming that relationship can bring a whole set of problems on its own, but what really complicates things is if we try to use the Shared Matches tool with Jane.

Instead of pulling in matches from a single shared ancestral couple, say Russ and Peg, it will be pulling in shared matches from Joe's line as well. If you are unaware, it can cause big problems in your Plan.

Take-home: if you see a match who is sharing too many centimorgans, evaluate their pedigree for a double relationship.

189

pedigree collapse

Think about your family tree like an inverted triangle, with you at the bottom and your ancestors fanning

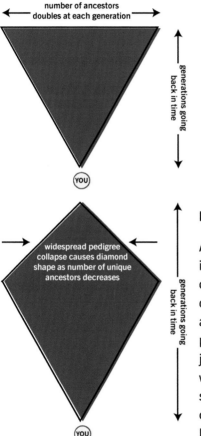

out above you. You go quickly from two parents to four grandparents, eight great grandparents, 16 gg-grandparents, 32 ggg-grandparents, 64 gggg-grandparents, and so forth. By the time you get out to 10 generations, there are 1,024 spots for ancestors on your pedigree chart (YIKES - that's a lot of people to find!), and the numbers just keep doubling from there.

Except when they don't.

At some point in everyone's pedigree, instead of different individuals filling out your chain of generations, some of the same ancestors will start to appear multiple times. The term pedigree collapse does a very good job of describing this situation, as when repeat ancestors fill in pedigree slots the inverted triangle starts to collapse in on itself and look more like a diamond.

Although this scenario plays out in everyone's pedigree at some point, you need to pay attention if you are a genetic genealogist who has pedigree collapse in the most recent few generations. And by that I mean if you have cousins marrying cousins in the last 4 generations of your genealogy, you need to read this section.

In very general terms, when you have ancestors who are cousins marrying each other, the result is people in your DNA match list who are sharing more DNA than they should.

Case Study: Pedigree Collapse

Let's look at a case study to see just how an instance of pedigree collapse affects levels of DNA sharing between a couple of cousins. This example examines the question of whether an isolated incident of recent pedigree collapse would raise the amount of DNA shared by cousins enough to send up the red flag. Would this elevated figure tip them off that they have more than one relationship in their recent ancestry? Or will the level of DNA sharing still fall in the expected range for just one of their relationships?

Let's first take a step back and remind ourselves what we can expect from a regular family. If Adam and Anna have Betsy, and then Betsy has Charlie who marries unrelated Cindy, then Dan and Donna are siblings, Ethan and Eva first cousins, and Fred and Fiona second cousins. This is what you would expect in a regular family.

Now meet the Colapso family. Adam and Anna have two children, Bob and Betsy. These siblings marry spouses who are unrelated to the Colapso family and have their own children, Charlie and Cindy, who are first cousins. Things start to get interesting when these first cousins marry and have two children, Dan and Donna. Looking first at Dan, he has two parents (as we'd expect) and four grandparents, but instead of the expected eight different great-grandparents he has only six unique great-grandparents. He is related to Adam and Anna through both his dad and his mom. This is also true for Dan's sister, Donna, as well. She has only six great-grandparents and is related to Adam and Anna through both her mom and dad. Can you see the beginnings of the diamond shape of this collapsed pedigree?

So how does this change when Charlie and Cindy are first cousins? Well, essentially, it created TWO relationships for each of their descendants. Let's look at Ethan and Eva. They are first cousins through their parents Charlie and Cindy, AND third cousins through Adam and Anna.

As we learned in the centimorgan section (page 207) when reviewing family relationships, there is an expected average level of DNA shared between people with given relationships. It's also important to note that due to random inheritance, the further back the ancestor, the less likely that there are segments large enough in current descendants today to be detected by the types of methods currently used by ancestry testing companies. For instance, AncestryDNA estimates that only 32% of documented fifth cousins will share enough DNA inherited from their common ancestor for that relationship to be detected.

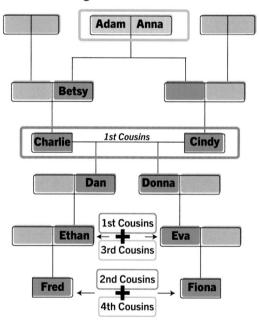

So let's take a look at those expected amounts for each of these family members (see the next page). All the numbers in the table come from the averages in the Shared cM Project (page 207).

Are you surprised by the result? I was.

If Ethan and Eva were to encounter each other for the first time on a DNA match list, this exercise tells us that their increased DNA sharing would likely not be enough to tip them off to the fact that there is a recent occurrence of pedigree collapse in their shared ancestry. They still look a lot like just regular 1st cousins—1st cousins whose recent ancestors are entirely unrelated.

	Relationship	Average shared cMs	Observed range of shared cM (from ScP)	Calculated shared cM (A+B)	Total shared cM reported by the testing company
	A	**A**	**A**		
Dan & Donna	Siblings	2629 cM	2209 - 3384	D&D: 2862	D&D: 2902
Ethan & Eva	1st Cousin	874 cM	553 - 1225	E&E: 948	E&E: 917
Fred & Fiona	2nd Cousin	233 cM	46 - 515	F&F: 268	F&F: 254
	B	**B**	**B**		
Dan & Donna	2nd Cousin	233 cM	46 - 515		
Ethan & Eva	3rd Cousin	74 cM	0 - 217		
Fred & Fiona	4th Cousin	35 cM	0 - 127		

The same is true for other, more distant, cousin relationships not nearly as close as our example, where the Colapso family had 1st cousins marrying and having children. The amount of shared DNA between 2nd cousins Fred and Fiona in the Colapso family is only elevated by a mere 35 cM on average, because we are adding an additional 4th cousin relationship (through Anna and Adam) through their 2nd cousin relationship through Cindy and Charlie. The shared DNA between Fiona and Fred is still compatible with the expected range of shared cM for second cousins without pedigree collapse.

The short of it: The effect of the pedigree collapse isn't always that significant to begin with, and it is certainly lessened with each succeeding generation, as descendants become more distant from the *double-dose* ancestors that appear twice in their pedigree.

Because this is one of the closest forms of isolated pedigree collapse possible (the union of 1st cousins to produce children would only be upstaged in genetic similarity by the union of siblings, half-siblings, uncle-niece, and other immediately related relative pairs), it follows that more distantly related unions (2nd cousin and so forth) would have even less of an effect on the total shared DNA between their descendants. So cousins resulting from these more distantly related unions who encounter each other for the first time on a DNA company match list would likely see no evidence of this kind of relationship.

Now, there are some other ways we can try to unravel these relationships. For example, using XDNA or YDNA, or even looking at some more advanced features of atDNA. But for most people, autosomal DNA is not very helpful at measuring pedigree collapse.

removed cousins

I know, I know, removed relationships can make your brain hurt. It just means someone who is in a different generation than you. This person is your parent's age, or your children's age.

Think of your first cousin. Do you have that person in mind? Now think of his child. That person, your first cousin's child, is your first cousin once removed. Removed relationships are labeled as 1C1R or 2C2R. This means first cousin once removed and second cousin twice removed, respectively.

> **Why don't I see removed relationships in my match list?** Based on the cM numbers as well as other factors, the testing company provides you with a range of relationship possibilities, like 2nd to 3rd cousins. Keep in mind that they are using genealogical terms to define a genetic relationship. Did you catch that? I said *that they are using genealogical terms to describe a genetic relationship.* While a genealogist interprets a second cousin as two people who are sharing one set of great grandparents, genetic second cousins could have several possible genealogical relationships, including 3rd cousins and 1st cousins once or twice removed. So what does this mean for you and your search? It simply means that when a company tells you someone is your second cousin, that doesn't actually mean they are your second cousin.

To determine your match's generation relative to your own, the only information you really have to go on to determine which generation they are in is their age. At MyHeritage and 23andMe, the age of your match is shown when they have turned it on in their preferences.

If you don't see their age right away, take a look at the parent generation in the pedigree of your match and see if you can find a year of birth. If the parent generation is marked *Private* that can often mean your match's parents are still alive. If you don't see birth years at the parent generation, move back to the grandparent generation.

Your goal here is to decide where you fit on their chart. Are you their age, their parents' age, or maybe their children's age? Put an "X" on their chart where you think you might fit. Then count generations forwards or backwards until you reach your match's place on the chart. However many generations you had to move, that's how *removed* you are from them. If you are the same age, as in this first example, then you are on the same generation. That means that if you are second cousins, one of your sets of great grandparents (any set) would be the same as one of his sets of great grandparents (any set).

In the second example on the next page, in the Best Mystery Match's (let's call him Matthew) family tree you can see that his parents were born in 1947. You were born in 1945. So you would put an "X" on Matthew's parents' generation, then count one generation to the left before you run into Matthew. So, you and Matthew are *once removed.* So now when we are looking at shared ancestors, we have to go back one generation farther in Matthew's tree before we find a common ancestor. You can read more about this in the Finding the Generation of Connection resource on page 147.

One of the biggest problems with understanding removed relationships

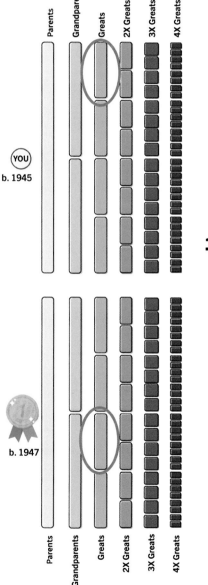

196

is that removed can go both ways. The above example described someone younger than you being your first cousin once removed. But we can think of it the other way. Think of your mom's first cousin (so the child of your mom's aunt or uncle). That person is also your first cousin once removed.

So a 1C1R (first cousin once removed) can be older than you, or younger than you. It gets even trickier when we start talking about people who are two times removed! But all of this removing does show itself, albeit subtly, in your DNA. For example, if someone is sharing 78 cMs with you, the testing company will likely call them your third cousin, as 3rd cousins share 75 cMs on average. However, if you are 80 and the match is 20, it is very unlikely that you are true third cousins. It is much more likely that you have another relationship that also shares about 72 cMs. Looking at the ScP table (see page 97) we see that second cousins twice removed (2C2R) also share that amount of DNA. So if you are 80, someone who is twice removed would be the same age as your grandkids. So that fits!

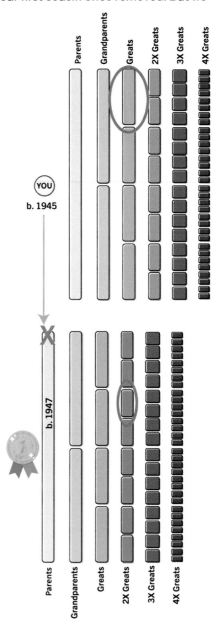

Occasionally, your reckoning will be off if there was a considerably large or small gap between a generation on your side or your match's. For example, say your grandma was the youngest-by-far child in a family of eight children. It's possible the oldest child was already a parent by the time she came around, or at least that she had nieces and nephews about her own age. Another scenario would be if motherhood came at a relatively young age for a couple of generations (a sequence of two fifteen-year old mothers can decrease the generation gap significantly!), or a 60-year old man fathered a son. Watch for these possibilities by keeping an eye on the birth years of each generation.

Do you see how taking that shared amount of DNA, and then adding in the age of the people tested as just one other bit of information can change the way you see your relationship? This is all with the goal of helping determine your generation of connection (see page 147).

This all works just swimmingly until you see a match whose parents were born in 1959. With you in 1945, it can be unclear where you fit in. In that case, start with the easiest route: theorize that you and your match are the same generation. You can always adjust later when you get more information.

But no matter what numbers you see, you need to just make your best guess about where you might fit in. So, don't go back to your Plan until you have decided if you and your Best Match are in the same generation, or once or twice removed.

Once you have your best guess in hand, head back to your Plan.

research log

Just because you are doing DNA research instead of paper research does not mean you get to bounce around willy-nilly and not carefully record all you are doing. If you are already using good research practices in your regular genealogy work, fantastic. Keep it up. If you want a few tips, this is how I do it.

Your research log consists of the *when*, *where*, and *why* of your research. This is your brain and your memory bank. Even if you think you will remember something later, you won't unless you write it down. For example, when we were newly married starving college students my mom would fly in for a visit and our first stop on the way home was Costco so she could buy meat to stock our freezer. She was the daughter of a grocer and had learned young how to package meat, so when we got home we would portion out all the protein and label each package with the contents and the date.

I was packaging ground beef, but I got tired of writing *hamburger* so instead I wrote just *ham* on one package, thinking that surely later I would know what was inside. Do I even need to tell you the rest of the story? How I saw the package in the freezer months later and was delighted about all the things I could cook with my ham?

Yeah...

Don't skip this step, it just saves a lot of duplication and ultimately head-smacking when you realize you just spent two hours doing something you had already done.

So, for DNA purposes, your research log should look something like this:

Date

Testing Company

Started in [ThruLines] to find a Best Match who is a descendant of [Name of Ancestor you are researching].

Used [Best Match Name] to run Shared Matches. Labeled all shared matches down to [20 cM] with the [purple] dot labeled [Murphy + Untch].

Went back to [ThruLines] and used [Best Match #2 Name] to run Shared Matches. Labeled all shared matches down to [20 cM] with the [purple] dot labeled [Murphy + Untch].

Noticed that [Match Name] already had a pink dot, which means we may be related more than once. Left both dots, but will not be using [Match Name] for Shared Matches.

You get the picture, right? Just write down everything you are doing, everyone you are labeling, and every idea that comes into your head. For the purposes of this book, **I also recommend making note of the step in the Plan you are on when you were making the notes**. This will help you come back on another day and pick up where you left off.

But even more importantly than that, writing down your process forces you to organize your thoughts. Many times this will lead to a discovery of a pattern in your matches that you might have otherwise overlooked.

searching by surname and location

If you are trying to figure out how a match is related to you, or just trying to gather more matches for your genetic network, you can use the surname and location tools to help.

Each of our ancestors has three key pieces of information that we can use to find them: Names, Locations, and DNA. This whole book is about taking the genetic approach to finding and using the key DNA matches that can lead you to your ancestors. But that doesn't mean we can't use a more low-tech way to find the information we are looking for.

Each of our testing companies allows you to search by surname and location in their match pages. So go for it! Look for the search box or icon at the top of your match page at any company and see if you can find some key matches by just doing a simple search.

In addition, if you know your ancestor was from Germany, you can look for other matches who have German heritage, or who live in Germany now. Read on to learn what kinds of surname and location tools each company offers.

23andMe

In the DNA match list there is a sidebar where you can search for ancestor birthplaces. You can also click on any match to compare your user-entered family locations as well as compare your ethnicity percentages vs. theirs.

AncestryDNA

There are several ways to search your AncestryDNA results by surname and location.

In the DNA Story ethnicity section: If you belong to any Genetic Communities (designated with the dotted line, see page 13) you can click on that place to see just a couple of your matches who belong to the same Genetic Community (if you have one).

In the main DNA match page: Simply use the search button at the top of the page to search by match name, or by a surname that appears in anyone's tree.

Clicking on any match brings up the individual match profile page with several ways you can view shared surname and location information.

Surnames Section: Scrolling down from the main pedigree view you will see the interactive Surnames section where you can view any shared surnames between you and your match, as well as just a list of the surnames that appear in their tree. All the surnames are clickable links that pull up the names of the actual ancestors for comparison.

Ancestor Birth Locations: This interactive map shows any locations that overlap between you and your DNA match. Clicking on a location will pull up a list of your ancestors and your match's ancestors that lived in that place.

Ethnicity tab: Under the header on the match profile page you will see three tabs: Trees, Ethnicity, and Shared Matches. Clicking on the Ethnicity tab brings up a comparison of your ethnicity results, as well as an indication of your shared genetic communities, if you have them.

Family Tree DNA

At the top of the Family Finder match page you can search your match list by surname. The match box does not search pedigree charts, only information that has been entered and displayed on the match page. So if your match has added some surnames and locations to their account, and they are showing up in the far right column, those are fair game for the search.

LivingDNA

At the top of the Family Matching results page there is a search box where you can search by surname or location. For many of your matches, you will also see a little flag icon next to their profile picture. This indicates the location where this match was born.

MyHeritage DNA

There are several places in the MyHeritage DNA website where you can view information about surnames and locations. The best place to start is in the *Overview* tab. There you will find:

Locations: In this map and list are the locations of where your DNA matches live. The list is interactive, so you can click on a location to see all of the matches who are from that place.

Ethnicities: Similarly, you can click on a list of all of the reported ethnicities at MyHeritage, and how many of your DNA matches fall into each category. Clicking on the number will bring up a list of matches who all have that location in their ethnicity report.

Then in the main match page, you can just click on the search button in the upper right of the match page to search your DNA match list by name or ancestral surname.

If you click on *Filters* at the top of the match page on the right you will see an option to filter your list by:

All tree details: which will allow you to filter by shared surnames or shared places (among other things).

All locations: which is just another way to get to the locations list mentioned above in the Overview.

All ethnicities: again, another way to see the ethnicity information you can see in the Overview section.

segment size

When talking about pieces of DNA and pieces of pie, the same adage applies: the bigger the better! In short: bigger pieces of DNA mean closer relationships. Now if you are working with close DNA matches, you can pretty much ignore this section, because when you have close matches, they are all sharing a ton of DNA in a bunch of big pieces.

But there are two situations where you will certainly want to turn to segment length to give you some clues to your relationships: When you are looking for a 2X or 3X great grandparent, or when you are thinking there might be some endogamy at play.

Going After Greats

If you are after your 3X great grandmother and dealing with a bunch of 4th cousins, you need to pay attention. Part of the problem with trying to find an ancestor so far back using your DNA is that you don't even have that much DNA from that ancestor, let alone share it with other descendants of her. Plus, your DNA has had a long ride being passed down generation after generation, and it might be in pretty rough shape. Meaning, you might not have very much of it to work with. But even with all of that going on, you still seem to have an abundance of DNA fourth cousin matches.

So when you create your genetic network and you are faced with hours of genealogy building out the trees of your DNA matches, you want to be sure it is going to be worth it, and not all 4th cousin matches are created equally. You will want to work with those matches who not only share the most centimorgans, but also who have the biggest pieces. At the end of this section you will see instructions on how to access segment data for each company.

Some important points:

- Pieces of DNA under 10 cM are rarely *real*. Meaning, they are rarely pieces of DNA that were inherited by the both of you from a single recent common ancestor.

- Pieces over 20 cM are almost always real.

- At AncestryDNA you cannot see the size of the biggest piece of DNA, only the total number of segments. So when you are down in the woods of your 4th cousin matches, give greater emphasis to those with *fewer* segments. Yes, you read that right, *fewer* segments. For example, if you are sharing 20 cM with both Sue and George, but with George you share that 20 in one piece, but with Sue it is in 3 pieces, who is the better match? Right! It's George because we know he has a nice big 20 cM piece of DNA shared with you.

Endogamy
The ins and outs of endogamy are best understood by reading the entire resource page on this topic on page 130. But the short of it is, endogamy can often be recognized when you have a large amount of total shared DNA in lots of tiny pieces.

Here's how to find the size of the biggest piece of DNA data at each company:

MyHeritage and FTDNA
At MyHeritage and Family Tree DNA they make this number very easy to find. The size of your longest block is displayed right there on your main match page. It is on the right under *DNA Match Quality*. To see more segment information, you can open the chromosome browser tool (page 114).

23andMe
At 23andMe it is a bit more complicated. To find out more about segment

sizes you will need to use the chromosome browser. Check out page 114 to learn more.

AncestryDNA

As mentioned, AncestryDNA does not share segment size, nor do they have a chromosome browser for us to check segment sizes. What they do provide is the number of pieces of shared DNA and you can see that information on the main match page, or at the top of an individual match profile page.

shared centimorgan project

Some of the sites provide interpretive tools to help you identify what your genetic relationship might be to your match. Another important tool is the Shared Centimorgan Project (ScP). The ScP provides much of the same information you can get from Ancestry's tool (page 103), but it isn't always the same. So even if you are working in Ancestry, the ScP is a great tool to have.

The ScP was headed up by genetic genealogist Blaine Bettinger and then refined and posted on the DNA Painter website by Leah Larkin and Jonny Perl. You can see more about this project at www.yourDNAguide.com/scp.

Essentially, the project asked real people like you how much DNA they share with their known cousins. All of those varying cM amounts were gathered into one place, giving us some interesting insight into the association between the cM numbers and different kinds of cousins.

Here's how it works:

1. Put the total amount of DNA you are sharing with a match you want to research in the box at the top of the page.

2. A table will appear showing the most likely relationships you could have with that match based only on the amount of DNA you are sharing.

3. Also note that in the chart under the table, all the unavailable relationships have been dimmed.

One of the very most insightful things about the ScP is that it documents the absolutely crazy and unpredictable way that DNA is inherited. For example, it is reported in the ScP that on average third cousins share about 75 cMs. But the ScP saw true third cousins who didn't share any

DNA, and others who shared a whopping 217 cMs! Essentially that means that any genealogical relationship that doesn't have a zero probability is a genetic possibility. (Doesn't that phrase sound like something you should cross-stitch on a pillow?)

While it is important to realize that these numbers tell a story about your relationship with another person, it is equally important to realize that **the story of just one match can be very different than that of another**. Let's say that two siblings have tested and you match them both (see page 138). With one you are sharing 175 cM. According to the ScP that could make you second cousins, and with just that one test, you might be wondering why you can't identify your shared great grandparents. But then with the other sibling you are sharing only 42 cMs — an amount that paints a very different picture of your relationship. Either one of these matches on their own may lead you in the wrong direction. But together you can realize the possible range of your shared connection (anywhere from 2nd to 4th cousins), and conduct your research accordingly.

208

Bottom line here: This total amount of DNA may not precisely identify your genealogical relationship, but it helps define the generation in which you and your match need to start looking for your common ancestor. We will refer to this throughout this book as the generation of connection.

shared matches tool

The Shared Matches tool is just a filter that helps you find matches in your match list that can help you with your question. All of our testing companies provide this tool. At the end of this section you will see how to access this tool at each of the DNA testing companies.

Using the Shared Matches tool starts with identifying your Best Match. Your Plan will help you find the right person to start with. Using Shared Matches on this Best Match will provide you with a subset of your match list. The people on this list are sharing DNA with you AND with your Best Match. **We call this group a genetic network.**

Theoretically, this means that all of the people on the list share a common ancestor with each other. For example, if you and your Best Match share 2X great grandparents Earl and Elizabeth, all of your matches should either be descendants of Earl and Elizabeth, or descendants of Elizabeth's ancestors or Earl's ancestors.

However, just the fact that you are all sharing DNA with each other does NOT mean that you are all part of one big happy family that shares a single common ancestor. Unfortunately, it's just not that simple. Let's explore this idea a bit further.

Why Shared Matches Appear

There are three reasons people may show up on your Shared Matches list:

ONE: They are actually related to you and your Best Match through a single recent common ancestor. This is what we are hoping for! You'll know this is the case when you identify that common ancestor by actually doing genealogy.

TWO: You are from a small community.

To explain this possibility, let's go back to your 2X great grandparents Earl and Elizabeth that you share with your Best Match, whom we will call Bill. When you look at your shared matches with Bill, you see Henry, Larry, and Joan. Remember, all the Shared Matches tool tells us is that all these people are sharing DNA with you and with Bill. When you look at their family trees, you see that each of these three matches is related to you in different ways—not through a single common ancestral line. Similarly, they are all related to Bill in different ways.

So how can you tell if your Shared Matches list is representing a connection to a single recent ancestor (or ancestral couple), or just a community? It helps to first identify your generation of connection (see page 147) for each match. If you know all of your ancestors on that generation of connection, but you don't see any shared ancestors with your match, it might be due to this problem of small communities. But don't worry, your Plan will walk you through all of that when it's time, I just wanted to give you a heads up.

THREE: You are related to your Best Match in multiple ways. We cover this scenario in more detail on page 187. But in general, if you and your match are related through more than one ancestor, this whole shared matches thing is not going to work like we planned, especially if the multiple relationships are in a recent generation. If you already know this is true (or begin to suspect it is true because everyone seems to share DNA with everyone else when you begin labeling), read that Multiple Relationships section referenced above for further instructions.

Finding Shared Matches at Your Testing Company
Here's how to find the Shared Matches tool at each company:

23andMe: Click on a match; scroll down until you see *Common Matches*.

AncestryDNA: Click on your Best Match, then on the tab *Shared Matches*. At AncestryDNA this list will only include individuals who are 4th cousins or closer to BOTH you and this Best Match. That means if you are searching for a 3X great grandparent, there may be some 4th cousins who aren't quite meeting AncestryDNA's 4th cousins threshold (just because they aren't sharing enough DNA with both of you). So you may want to look for more matches using the Surname and Location searches. See page 201.

Family Tree DNA: Click on the box next to a Best Match. Click on the *In Common With* button at the top of the match page.

Living DNA: On your dashboard, click *Ancestry*, then *Family Matches*.

MyHeritage: Click on *Review Match Details*, then scroll down until you see *Shared Matches*. However, you will only be able to see this list if you have met certain requirements:

1. You purchased a DNA test from MyHeritage and have an active *MyHeritage Premium* or *Premium Plus* subscription.

2. You transferred your DNA to MyHeritage from another testing company and you paid the $29 unlock fee.

211

So...what are you waiting for? Get out there and find the shared matches for your Best Match.

Now head back to your Plan to see what is next.

strategy: ask the wife

So you have created a genetic network that has helped you identify a family to whom you are likely related. Congratulations! But because DNA is unpredictable, you can't be quite certain of where exactly you fit in this family. You need more information.

Let's go over an example. Let's say your Best Match is Erin. By using Match Blocks and the Generation of Connection (see page 180 and page 147 respectively) you think that Erin is your second cousin, or second cousin once removed. That means that your shared ancestors with Erin are either one set of her four great grandparents, or one set of her eight 2X great grandparents.

Using the Shared Matches tool and the principles of creating a genetic network (see page 209) you found a group of matches who connect to Erin in her Longden line (Alex, Bob, and Carl are all Longdens). This is a

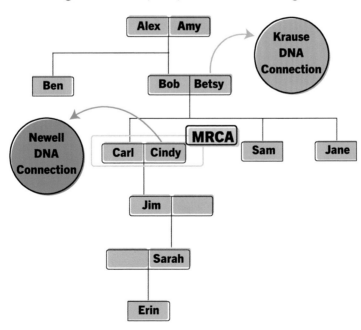

significant boost to your research as this tells you that your connection with Erin can most likely be found either in Carl and Cindy Longden, her great grandparents, or in Bob and Betsy Thomas, her 2X great grandparents.

Let's review the principles you learned from creating a genetic network that helped us learn of your connection to the Longden family.

You used the Shared Matches tool on Erin and found three 4th cousins who all connect to Alex and Amy Longden, the parents of Bob, Erin's 2X great grandfather. So at the very least, you can be fairly confident that you are a descendant of Alex and Amy.

But I am guessing that isn't going to be enough for you. So, we need to Ask the Wife! You see, if you are a descendant of Bob and Betsy, you should have Betsy's DNA as well, correct? That means you should have another genetic network in your DNA match list that represents Betsy's family. Let's say her maiden name was Krause. So you are looking in your match list for a group of people who share DNA with each other and have a Krause ancestor in their family tree (specific instructions on how to do this will be given in The Plan for your individual DNA Journey).

Let's say you find that connection to the Krause family. Because you can see that the Krause genetics met up with the Longden genetics at Bob and Betsy, you can add them to your list of likely ancestors. This means that you are a descendant of Bob and Betsy through one of their children.

Now that we have that sorted out, we can move down to the next generation. Here we are asking if Erin's ancestors Carl Longden and Cindy Newell are your ancestors, or if you are a descendant of one of Carl's siblings.

What do we do? We Ask The Wife!

If you are a descendant of Carl and Cindy, you should have a genetic network in your DNA match list that corresponds to the Newell family.

So, you go out and look (again, specific instructions will be found in your Plan) and sure enough, you see a connection to the Newells through a handful of third cousins. And there you have it! You have just figured out how you are related to Erin. You are both descendants of Carl Longden and Cindy Newell.

Now, what if you didn't see a connection to the Newells? Well, then you need to examine the spouses of all of Carl's siblings. The strategy is called *Ask The Wife*, but really it should be *Ask The Spouse* (it just doesn't have quite the same ring to it). You could be a descendant of any of Carl's brothers or sisters. To find out which one, you need to examine your DNA match list for a genetic network that connects you to one of the spouses of those Longden siblings.

Make sense?

OK, let's get back to your Plan and get to work.

214

strategy: bottoms up

Ok, so you have yourself a genetic network. You made it either by employing one of the Strategies in this book or by using a Known Match and the Shared Matches Tool.

Now you want to split this genetic network into smaller genetic networks. Remember, every genetic network you have can be parsed out into smaller and smaller groups. We use this Bottoms Up strategy when we have a group of people representing an ancestral *couple*, but what we want is the DNA matches that pertain to just *one ancestor*, either the husband or the wife in that identified couple. You know, when you have matches related to your great grandparents Joseph and Jane, but you only want to research Jane.

To find the Bottom (this is essential, you'll see), the first question you need to ask yourself is, **what kinds of cousins can BEST help me find my ancestor?**

If you are looking for your 3X great grandparent, other descendants of that unknown ancestor and their spouse will be your 4th cousins, right? (Trust me, that's how it works). So the matches that will best help you find your ancestor will be 4th cousins.

All right, so you have identified your Bottom (he, he, sorry, had to laugh, maybe it's because I have teenage boys?): the kind of cousins you need to answer your question. Now time for the step-by-step guide to using this Bottoms Up Strategy. Consider yourself reminded that you need to write all of this stuff down in your Research Log.

1. Take a look at the matches in your genetic network. Scroll all the way to the bottom of your Bottom category. So if the matches that will be most helpful are 2nd cousins, then scroll to the end of your second cousin list. This is pretty straightforward at Ancestry, but at the other companies there are lots of

relationship ranges that can make it hard to see the category definitions. So you may want to review the chart on page 180 that gives some loose guidelines on how much DNA each relationship will share, and make your own categories within your match page.

2. All right, so you are at the bottom of your Bottom. If you are in the 2nd or 3rd cousin category, inch up maybe one or two matches. There! That's the match I want! If you are looking at 4th cousins, read the guidelines for choosing a good 4th cousin match at the end of this section, then jump back in this process at step 4.

3. Label that match with the match's name (see page 176).

4. Then use the Shared Matches tool (page 209) on them to find and label a genetic network surrounding this match. This means that some of the matches you had already labeled in your first go-around will get a second label (this is good).

5. Now go back to your original genetic network list. Scroll down again to the bottom of Bottom until you see the match you were just working with. Move up the list until you see a match that does not have two labels.

6. Run the Shared Matches tool on that match, and label all the matches you find.

7. Keep doing this until all the matches in your original network have at least two labels.

In case you want to know: Why the bottom of the Bottom? Well, it is really because the edges of each category are the most wishy-washy. Meaning that at the bottom of the 2nd cousin list are actually some 2C1R and some 1C2R, etc. These kinds of matches can complicate our analysis at times, so it is safest to start with a match in the middle-ish. So maybe I should have called it the middle-up strategy? But that just doesn't sound as catchy.

Here's an example. Let's say you are trying to find your 2X great grandmother Wilma's parents (so your hole is your 3X greats). You used a cheat to find Denise, your Known Match, as she is a descendant of Wilma through one of her other children. You then use Shared Matches on Denise and have gathered a nice genetic network.

Now, Denise is your 3rd cousin and shares 68 cM with you. Using Shared Matches on her will gather all of your siblings, first cousins, and second cousins who are also descendants of Wilma. Those people are not very helpful, even if you aren't sure who they are. Anyone in the first, second and likely even third cousin categories will be sharing too much DNA with you to be descendants of Wilma's siblings.

Your Best Mystery Match will be a 4th cousin. Why? Because we are looking for a match who can lead us to Wilma's parents. People who are descendants of Wilma's parents (so descendants of Wilma's siblings) will be your fourth cousins.

So your Best Mystery Match should be a fourth cousin—likely someone in your genetic network who is sharing less DNA than Denise. So I would go to the genetic network with Denise. Scroll to the bottom of the 4th cousin list, and then using the tips at the end of this section, I would choose a 4th cousin match to start with. Then use the Shared Matches tool on this match, and label them with the name of this match.

Then I would go back to my network with Denise, find the next match, and repeat the process until everyone in the original network has two labels. Got it?

OK, what next?

Do genealogy! Each of these new two-dotted genetic networks should have a common ancestor with each other. But I am getting ahead of myself. Go back to your Plan for the next steps.

Troubleshooting:

Problem: I don't see more than one group within my original group.

To Do: It may be because the Bottom match you used to create the network is actually related to you more closely than you suspect. Good thing you kept that research log, right? Go back and review the matches you used to create the new networks. Look for possible double relationships. Remove the dots created by any suspicious matches (those you think might be related in multiple ways).

To Do: The ancestral couple who created your original network is related to each other. We call this endogamy, or pedigree collapse. The short of it is—I hate to say it—this is going to be HARD. You can try to move on in the Plan with this large group, and just try to use genealogy strategies to sort things out, but prepare yourself: DNA may not be the answer you were hoping for.

So? How did that go? OK? Good. Now head back to your Plan to see what is next.

Guidelines for choosing a good 4th cousin match

If you have identified 4th or 5th (yikes - you are sure you want to do this with 5th cousins?!) cousins as your Bottom, then we need to have a little chat before I set you lose with all the labeling.

Matches at this level are notoriously unpredictable. Not all of these matches represent connections to real shared ancestors. Some of them are sharing DNA with you not because you share a recent common ancestor, but because you come from a common population group. So we want to choose matches that are more likely to represent real connections.

So when trolling your Bottom list from the bottom, look for a match who is sharing the largest segments (or at Ancestry, has the fewest segments). Read all about segments on page 204. Use that match to jump back into the step-by-step process above at step #3.

strategy: cousin categories

You were all excited to get going using your DNA to find your ancestor, but you are actually missing quite a few ancestors, and you don't have a Best Known Match for the line you are trying to research. That's ok, we can still try to find out more about your ancestor.

To get started, the first question you need to ask yourself is, **what kinds of cousins can BEST help me find my ancestor?**

If you are looking for your grandparents, great grandparents, or 2X great grandparents (this strategy is not recommended for relationships further back than this), other descendants of that unknown ancestor and their spouse will be your 1st cousins/2nd cousins/3rd cousins, right? (Trust me, that's how it works). So the matches in the match category that will best help you find your ancestor will be your 1st cousins/2nd cousins/3rd cousins.

Here's the step-by-step to use this strategy to help you find your Best Mystery Match, so we can keep going with the Plan:

1. Take a look at the 1st cousin/2nd cousin/3rd cousin category (again, which category you look at depends on your question) in your DNA Match list. This is pretty straightforward at Ancestry, but at the other companies there are lots of relationship ranges that can make it hard to see the category definitions. Basically, everyone sharing over 500 cM is in the first cousin category, between 150-499 are in the second cousin category, and from about 50-149 are third cousins. So go into your match list and draw your (somewhat arbitrary) category lines.

2. If you know how any of the cousins in this match category are related to you, use the Shared Matches tool as outlined on page 209 using this Known Match as your Best Match. Do this for

every Known Match in your target category (it's ok if you don't have any Known Matches).

3. Find a match in this target category who does not yet have a label.

4. Use the Shared Matches tool on this match, and label them with this match's name.

5. Repeat for any other matches in this category that do not have a label.

OK, time to stop and think for a second. Remember the match groups we discussed as part of our discussion of genetic networks (for a refresher, see the glossary under genetic networks)? Remind yourself of how many match groups should be present for the generation you are focused on:

> Grandparents make TWO groups of first cousins
>
> Great grandparents make FOUR groups of second cousins
>
> 2X great grandparents make EIGHT groups of third cousins

Take a look at your list. Do you have the appropriate number of groups represented in the category you are focused on? If not, it could be for one of two reasons: one of your lines doesn't have anyone tested; two of your lines are related two each other (so they show up genetically as one). Don't worry too much about this right now, but keep these ideas in the back of your mind in case you need to pull them out later.

Your next step is to work with each of these genetic groups of matches to try to figure out how they are related to you, hoping that one of these networks represents the line you are specifically interested in. So quickly scan through the genealogy of each match group, looking for surname and location clues that might help you figure out if this is a line on which you want to focus. **If you can't see anything that looks familiar, it means you need to start working with this match group.** If your matches are lacking in family trees, try the resources on page 163 and page 141 to try to expand those trees a bit.

Now head back to your plan with this focus match group in mind. Your Best Mystery Match is the match in this match group who has the most shared DNA, and is in this target generation range.

What do I mean by that?

Well, when you used the Shared Matches tool on one of your mystery matches in your focus category, you were shown matches that were closer than this category. Like if your focus category is 3rd cousins, your shared matches will show some second cousins.

Don't use these second cousins as your Best Mystery Match! Use someone from the 3rd cousin category.

OK, off with you! Back to your Plan to see what is next.

strategy: leftovers

You are coming to this page with one of two woes:

A. Due to your question constraints or lack of DNA matches you haven't been able to find a Known Match in order to get started (poor you!).

B. You have created a genetic network that has helped you identify a family to whom you are likely related, but either because the records are spotty or we are dealing with some illegitimacy, you can't go poking around in your DNA match list looking for a specific name.

In either case, you are here because you have to take a purely genetic approach.

Most often **this means that you will need to group and label your entire match list with the information that you know**. Check out the step-by-step below.

What should happen after this process is that you will be left with a smallish group of matches who have no label. That means that they are related to your unknown line, and you can re-enter your Plan armed with the information you need to begin your research again.

When re-entering the Plan, use the match in your Leftovers group that has the most shared DNA as your Best Mystery Match. Before you head back to your Plan, write down in your research log (see page 199) an entry for this Best Mystery Match. List their name, the total amount of DNA you are sharing, and any other details you find important.

Leftovers Strategy Two-Step

1. Using the cheating tools when possible (see page 105), identify your closest DNA matches for whom you know your relationship. So, if the ancestor you are looking for is on your dad's side, start by choosing your closest maternal match, and using

the Shared Matches tool (see page 209) to find everyone in your match list who is related to your mom. Make sure you label those matches (see page 176).

2. Repeat this process to label any paternal matches that you know, using the same genetic networks process. Simply put, you find a Best Known Match, use the Shared Matches tool, and add labels. You do that over and over and over again until you have labeled everyone you can on your match list. Make sure you are taking careful notes and writing everything down in your research log (see page 199).

Tip: When using the cheats like ThruLines, quickly check to make sure the genetic relationship agrees with the genealogy relationship of your match before you use the Shared Matches tool to gather and label others. See checking genetics vs genealogy for more details (page 111).

If at the end of this Leftovers process you do not see any matches without labels, you have likely encountered one of the following situations:

A. No other descendants of this line have taken a DNA test yet. (In the United States, where consumer DNA testing is strongest, perhaps your missing ancestor was an immigrant, who left behind other relatives in the Old Country, where descendants today are less likely to have tested.) What to do: Wait until the right person tests, or try targeted testing (page 224).

B. You may have used a match in the Shared Matches process who was not related in the way you thought they were. What to do: Go back and review your research log. Look for matches who either have too much or too little DNA for their suspected relationship. Remove all labels for that ancestor and try labeling them again, but this time without using that match.

C. Your missing ancestor is related to one of your other known ancestors, or at least to their population group. We call this en-dogamy, which means—I hate to say it—this is going to be HARD. Try the Getting Unstuck strategies on page 171, but prepare yourself: DNA may not be the answer you were hoping for.

Back to Mystery Match   Back to KM.43   Back to MM.28   Back to GN.22
Back to TOC

targeted DNA testing

Sometimes, all the DNA data at your current disposal isn't enough to help you answer the question on your mind. Maybe your Best Matches aren't responding, or despite your best efforts, you can't build the tree connections with existing records and trees.

So what if you could handpick a new Best Known Match? A specific descendant who just hasn't tested yet, whose DNA test might contain the answer to your mystery? You can try it. This practice is called targeted testing.

For example, let's say you have narrowed your search for your 2X great grandfather down to a group of Wilsons who lived in North Carolina. But they had lots of kids who had lots of kids, and it is really hard to tell which one is your ancestor. With your current group of DNA matches all being 4th cousins, there really isn't any more they can tell you about your relationship to this family.

With targeted testing, you'll likely have to research the descendants of your most likely ancestors and identify their living kin (see the section on Descendancy Research on page 161). Then you'll have to find contact information for those living strangers (see the section on Finding Living People on page 141), and ask him or her to take a DNA test.

Once you get to that point of first contacting your unknown kin, here are three tips:

1. Tell the story. You need to come up with a very succinct way to help your potential cousin understand what it is you are trying to accomplish. Write out two to three (compelling!) sentences that explain why this ancestor has been so elusive.

2. Help them see their role. You need to clearly communicate that it is pretty amazing that they, this living person today, can

help you unlock a mystery that is decades old. Help them feel that they have a particular mix of DNA that could likely provide answers where traditional documents just can't.

3. Tell them the risks. It is oh-so-important that your cousin fully understands what DNA testing can do: reveal relationships. You need to be very clear that taking a DNA test will reveal any biological relationships they have. You may want to download a consent form like the one provided by my dear friend Blaine Bettinger at https://tinyurl.com/GGconsent. This will help facilitate this conversation with your potential DNA cousin and make sure all your i's are dotted and t's are crossed.

225

tell your story

You have reached the end of this particular Plan and the end of that particular journey. I hope you feel a sense of accomplishment. As I attend conferences all over the world, I am constantly amazed at you: extraordinary people with a fierce passion for your family. You spend so much of your time, energy, and resources to seek out those who have come before you. More than ever, I find your passion contagious, and I want to know more about my people.

But it isn't enough just to know.

We have to share.

These stories must be told. I was in a large auditorium once when Judy Russell (the Legal Genealogist) was speaking. She had the entire audience stand up. Then she quizzed us on how much we knew about our ancestors. If you didn't know the answer, you would have to sit down. Slowly, one by one, the entire audience began to sit down as Judy progressed from simple questions about names and dates to more probing questions about hobbies and personalities.

Until we all sat.

But we were now sitting a little less comfortably because we knew that there was a story left untold.

So whatever story your DNA has just helped you tell, make sure you share it. Write it down. Tell your friends and your family. Put your newfound relatives on your tree, citing DNA and other evidence that connects you. Put images of your ethnicity results (even if they're not totally reliable) and Genetic Communities into a family history book, with your comments about them. Let's leave fewer stories untold than did the generation before us.

unless...

So, you have used your DNA sleuthing skills to identify your relationship to a DNA match. Great job! You did it!

Unless...you didn't.

It is very important to realize that there are always multiple genetic explanations for why two people share a certain amount of DNA. For example, let's take a set of two people sharing 1500 cM. They are the same age as each other. All signs point to a half-sibling relationship. However, that total amount of DNA doesn't have to be because of a single relationship. That same amount of DNA will be shared by people who have two relationships (see page 187). Perhaps they are actually double first cousins. An example of this is when two brothers marry two sisters. Their children become double first cousins. First cousins share about 800 cM; if we do that twice, we get 1600 cM.

All I am saying is, **BE CAREFUL**. Don't jump to any conclusions. Explore all the possibilities. And always, always verify with more research. Talk to family members, or look at genealogical records, or collect and analyze more DNA matches.

OK, head back to your Plan. I didn't mean to rain on your parade; I just wanted to be sure you brought your umbrella.

xDNA

Can XDNA help you with your DNA question? XDNA follows a unique inheritance pattern. It makes up your 23rd pair of chromosomes, which for men is XY and women is XX. Sometimes **XDNA is mistakenly thought of as maternal DNA**. This happens because a man gets his YDNA from his dad, and his XDNA from his mom. So anyone who is sharing XDNA with his mom has to be related on his mom's side. See — makes perfect sense that people think of it as maternal DNA. However, ladies get XDNA from *both* parents, making it uniparental (don't you hate how some people use big words just to make themselves look smart? Jeesh...).

Bottom line: XDNA is not just maternal DNA.

Take a look at these inheritance charts to help you keep straight which ancestors you get XDNA from, depending on if you are a man or a woman. In the images, the pink ancestors are female and the green ancestors are male. All of the varying shades of gray are ancestors from whom you do NOT get XDNA.

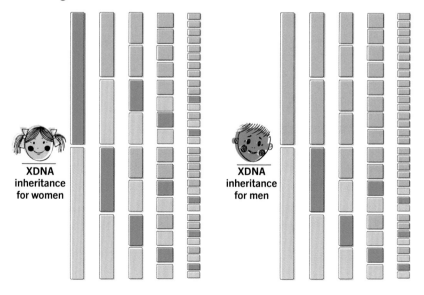

XDNA inheritance for women

XDNA inheritance for men

In spite of the confusion, XDNA can be a very valuable asset in specific cases in your genetic genealogy research. Since you are on this page, I am assuming that you have determined XDNA may be of some value to you. However, XDNA matching is only reported by two of the five DNA testing companies: 23andMe and Family Tree DNA. So if you haven't tested at either of these places, you can just skip this section and go back to your research plan. Or, you can keep reading. I guess I can't stop you. But if you can't use this information right now in the midst of your research goal, this is classified as a rabbit hole. One you could get stuck down. Just sayin'.

Finding XDNA data at 23andMe

23andMe doesn't make it very easy to find matches who are sharing on the XDNA. In fact, you have to look at each match one by one to evaluate them for the XDNA match. The easiest way to do this is to click on the match and then scroll down to the section called *your genetic relationship*. Click on the *Show DNA Details* link and that will expand the window to display the chromosome browser. (That is the image of your 23 chromosomes with colored stripes on it.) Look all the way to the right to see if you have a purple stripe on the chromosome marked "X."

Finding XDNA data at Family Tree DNA (FTDNA)

FTDNA gives you lots of options when it comes to finding which of your matches share XDNA with you. Probably the easiest is to load your main match page, and then click on the header labeled *XDNA* and it will sort your match list to show you all those sharing XDNA at the top.

Evaluating the shared XDNA

Even though I kind of just told you otherwise, all XDNA matches do not indicate that your shared ancestor has to be one highlighted in the chart. That's because most of your XDNA matches are not matching because you share a recent common ancestor, but because you just have some common pieces of XDNA.

To determine if your shared XDNA is actually pointing you to a specific shared ancestor, you need to find out how big your shared pieces are. You can do this by using the Chromosome Browser tool. Only the chromosome browsers at 23andMe and Family Tree DNA report XDNA information. Head over to page 114 to read all about chromosome browsing, then come back here to read this specific XDNA example from FTDNA.

Chromosome Browsing at FTDNA

Before you start: this isn't a section you can just read and understand. You have to be doing as I am doing. So put your bookmark in here, head over to your computer, login to FTDNA, and navigate to your Family Finder DNA match page.

I will wait here for you (patiently).

Ok, now we are ready! Start by sorting your matches by XDNA by clicking on the XDNA label at the top of the match page. For the first 8 matches, click on the box to the left of their name, and then choose the Chromosome Browser button from the section just above the match page.

A page will appear with the matches you have selected across the top. Note how each match has been assigned a color; this will be important in a second.

Right below your matches and their colors are a series of gray lines representing your 23 chromosomes. Occasionally sprinkled throughout the gray will be some colored lines indicating that at that spot on the chromosome, you and your match are sharing DNA. The color of the line corresponds to whichever match you are sharing that piece with.

Scroll all the way down to the bottom and check out the X chromosome. It is very possible that this chromosome is completely gray, or possibly has a few colored lines, but likely you won't see all eight of the individuals you added to this tool represented in the chart.

But wait a second, didn't the main match page indicate that all of these people were sharing XDNA? So, why don't you see a colored line? Well, it's because the piece of XDNA that they are sharing with you is smaller than the default threshold for the chromosome browser tool, which is set at 5 cM. To see the pieces you share, scroll back to the top and change the threshold using the dropdown menu to 1 cM. Now when you scroll down, what you see smattering your XDNA probably looks a lot like glitter.

Digression: My husband hates glitter. I think if he knew that having a darling baby girl meant glitter infiltrating every nook and cranny in our home, and getting stuck in his clothes and in his beard, he just may have declared her cute as a button, and then sent her back to wherever she came from.

These small pieces of shared XDNA are exactly like glitter: persistent bits of DNA that don't actually signal a relationship with a particular ancestor. If your shared piece of XDNA is below 10 cM, you can count it as glitter, and ignore the limitation that an XDNA match places on your possible pool of related ancestors. In short, you could still be related to this match through any ancestor, not just those who pass down the XDNA.

Now that you have this XDNA situation figured out, head back to your research Plan to see how all you have learned can impact your goal.

yDNA basics

Y chromosome DNA (YDNA) can only be taken by men and traces only a direct male line. YDNA testing should be investigated whenever you are looking for information about any man in your family tree. However, in order to use YDNA, you have to

find the right person to be tested. In general, that person is a living male who has the same surname as the person you are trying to research. Of course, if you come from a culture where the whole pass-the-surname-down tradition isn't a thing, then you need to adjust accordingly.

The YDNA test produces two kinds of results: a DNA match list and a haplogroup, or deep ancestral group. Both can be helpful in your genealogy research, but usually the match page is more so.

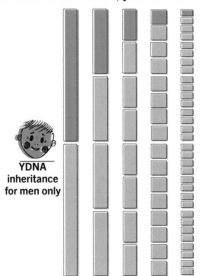

YDNA
inheritance
for men only

In the Lab

The two kinds of YDNA results are produced by two different kinds of DNA tests. Hapologroups are determined by testing single small changes in the DNA called SNPs (just say snips) while DNA matching measures repeating sections of DNA called STRs (no fun name here, just say all the letters).

The only company currently offering YDNA testing for matching purposes is Family Tree DNA. They offer three levels of testing: 37, 67, and 111, that correspond to the number of locations tested on the YDNA. **How many should you test?** It is safe to apply the more-is-better principle. However, often the 37 marker test is enough to tell you what you want to know: if you are or aren't related to another person. However, if you want to know for sure, or if you want to know how closely you are related, you need to test at 67. The 111 level is really more to help you refine your known relationships—to help you figure how exactly how several related lines may fit together.

Matching

The YDNA match page at FTDNA has a lot of information packed into a little bit of space. But in all this hub-bub, you really only need to **focus on two places: the genetic distance column, and the TiP calculator.**

Genetic Distance is a fancy way to describe the differences between the YDNA values of two men. Before you consider looking for a recent common paternal ancestor with a YDNA match, you want to find individuals who have 3 or fewer differences from your profile when you have tested at 37 or 67 markers. You can allow up to 5 differences at the 111 marker level. This rule really just ensures that you at least have a chance to find your common ancestor because he exists in a reasonable number of generations (like 8 or fewer).

The TiP calculator provides an estimate of how many generations back you would need to go before you can expect to run into your common ancestor. You can access it from your match table by clicking that orange button with the white "TiP" inside it. It will pull up a table like this one

COMPARISON CHART	
Generations	Percentage
2	16.70%
4	48.60%
6	70.93%
8	85.73%

that tells you how likely it is that you share a common ancestor in a given number of generations. In general, I like to start with the generation that has at least a 70% likelihood.

Haplogroups

Your haplogroup is your deep ancestral group. Each haplogroup can be associated with a different part of the world, sometimes even with specific population groups. Knowing the haplogroup of your paternal line can help you as you search databases and work to extend your paternal line genealogy.

If you belong to a common haplogroup you can expect to find many more false positive matches in the databases. These are matches that share many values with you, but are not recently paternally related.

The haplogroup assignment you received from FTDNA is just a prediction. They used the values in your profile to compare to a database of individuals with known haplogroups to determine yours. To definitively determine your haplogroup you need to have additional testing completed.

Two of our other companies, Living DNA and 23andMe, provide some of this additional testing as part of their autosomal DNA test. So if you are curious about your deep ancestral roots, you can head over to one of those companies and find out significantly more about your haplogroup.

Additional Testing

It addition to testing at 23andMe or Living DNA, there are other avenues to have more of your YDNA tested. Most notably is the BigY test at Family Tree DNA. That comprehensive test will dig deep into your YDNA, providing more SNPs and STRs than you can shake a stick at. This becomes especially useful if you are trying to piece together a paternal family relationship back in the 10-12 generation range.

The Short of It

YDNA is an essential part of any genetic genealogy plan. It is worth your time, effort, and funds to find the right person to be tested and see what the database can tell you.

Glossary

23andMe (www.23andme.com): One of the major consumer DNA testing companies, headquartered in California, U.S.A. Best known for its health reports (an optional purchase) and enormous testing pool, second only to AncestryDNA. page 7

AncestryDNA (www.ancestry.com/dna): The DNA test sold by genealogy website Ancestry.com, based in Utah, U.S.A. This testing company has the largest testing pool, but does not allow those who have tested elsewhere to transfer their results into their site. Has a wide range of tools to help build family trees and identify genealogical relationships to genetic matches. page 7

Autosomal DNA: Sometimes abbreviated atDNA, is shared by both your paternal and maternal relatives, and able to help quantify genealogical relatedness within the most recent 4-6 generations. This is the most common type of DNA testing, and is offered by 23andMe, AncestryDNA, Living DNA, MyHeritage DNA and (along with YDNA and mtDNA testing) by Family Tree DNA. page 7

Best Known Match: Someone who has a documented relationship to the ancestor you are trying to find. page 22

Best Mystery Match: A DNA match whose connection to you is unknown but who is your closest genetic match within a genetic network of interest, and preferably descends from a different child of an ancestral couple of interest OR your best DNA match for whom you don't know your relationship, but whom you can see is related to the line you want to research. page 23

Best Tree Match: The match in your genetic network who you can see has an ancestor in common with your Best Mystery Match. page 68, page 73

Centimorgan: The actual definition is complicated, but you can think of it as a unit of measure reflecting the amount of DNA you share with someone (in general, the more you share, the more closely you are related). page 103

Confirmation bias: When you have preconceived notions about an answer, so you judge the evidence based on how it fits with your theory instead of taking a more objective approach. page 124

Chromosome browser: A graphical representation of the DNA you share with your match. page 114

Endogamy: The practice by a community of marrying within its defined culture or location over and over and over again. page 130

Family Tree DNA (FTDNA, www.ftdna.com): One of the major consumer DNA testing companies; based in Texas, U.S.A. Known for providing YDNA and mtDNA tests as well as autosomal, and for providing information on XDNA. Also known for facilitating group projects, such as surname DNA studies or geographical studies. It allows users to upload from other companies. Their database is open to law enforcement, though you can opt out in your settings. page 7

Generation of connection: The generation in which you and your match need to look for your common ancestor. page 147

Genetic network: A group of people (generally, DNA matches) who all connect to you through a common ancestral couple. page 209

Haplogroup: A deep ancestral group assignment provided to YDNA and mtDNA test-takers, which gives broad, general information about where your paternal or maternal lines originated. **page 184, page 232**

Known Match: A DNA match who has a known genealogical relationship to you. **page 22**

Living DNA: www.livingDNA.com A consumer DNA testing company based in the U.K. Best known for detailed analysis of British Isles ancestral ethnicity. page 7

Mitochondrial DNA (mtDNA): DNA inherited only from your maternal side (your mother, her mother, her mother, etc.). This kind of DNA testing, for both women and men, can help identify matches on their maternal side but does not specify relatedness in sufficient detail as to describe exact genetic relationships. page 184

MRCA: Abbreviation for Most Recent Common Ancestor, or the closest ancestor that connects you to another person (so for your first cousin, the most recent common ancestors are your grandparents). page 22

MyHeritage DNA: www.myheritage.com The DNA test sold by genealogy website and Israeli-based company MyHeritage. This company has a wide range of tools to help build family trees and identify genealogical relationships to genetic matches. It also allows users to upload DNA test results from other companies. page 7

Mystery Match: A DNA match whose connection to you is unknown. page 40

New Mystery Match: A DNA match who belongs to a different genetic network than your Best Mystery Match. Hopefully a match whose line marries into the line of your Best Mystery Match. page 65

Pedigree collapse: When the same ancestors appear in more than one position on the family tree (such as when cousins marry cousins). page 190

Reference populations: Groups of people who have been chosen to genetically represent a population. page 13

Removed relationships: Genealogical relationships that are not on the same generation level (for example, your mother's first cousin is your first cousin one generation removed). page 195

Shared Centimorgan Project: Abbreviated in this book as ScP and found at www.dnapainter.com/tools. This tool helps you estimate the likelihood that you are related to a DNA match at a particular generation. page 207

Unlinked Tree: At AncestryDNA these are public trees that are in the account of your DNA match. However, your match has not linked themselves to the tree in the Ancestry system. This means that your match may or may not be the home person in the tree. You should look for unlinked trees in the accounts of your matches that DO have trees as well, as those additional trees may contain more/different information. page 73

XDNA: Has a unique inheritance pattern that can help you determine which lines a DNA match can be related through. page 228

YDNA: DNA inherited only from your paternal side (your father, his father, his father, etc.). This kind of DNA testing for men can help identify matches on their paternal side but does not generally specify relatedness in sufficient detail as to describe exact genetic relationships. page 232